Grammar
Step by Step

2

Helen Kalkstein Fragiadakis

Ellen Rosenfield

with Chants by Carolyn Graham

McGraw Hill

Dedicated to our families, with enormous gratitude
for their patience and support, and to our students, with
great appreciation for their inspiration over the years.

1 2 3 4 5 6 7 8 9 0 QPD 0 09

ISBN-13: 978-0-07-719757-5 (U.S. Edition)
ISBN-10: 0-07-719757-7 (U.S. Edition)
ISBN-13: 978-0-07-122030-9 (International Student Edition)
ISBN-10: 0-07-122030-5 (International Student Edition)

Cover designer: Delgado and Company, Inc.
Interior designer: Wee Design Group
Art: Tom Sperling / Elizabeth Wolf
Compositor: Page2, LLC

www.esl.mcgraw-hill.com

Audio Download Center

NEW... The Audio Download Center offers students the ability to access and download MP3 files for all of the listening activities and fun chants in the Student Book. All Audio Download Center content can be found by visiting **www.esl.mcgraw-hill.com/audio**.

Grammar Step by Step includes a wealth of listening activities that offer students practice in communicative competence while supporting the grammar lesson. The audio icon in the Student Book indicates when audio activities are available. All of the listening activities are available for the instructors on the Complete Audio CD Program that is packaged with the Teacher's Manual.

For a nominal fee, students can access and download MP3 files for *Grammar Step by Step* directly from the Audio Download Center at **www.esl.mcgraw-hill.com/audio**. Select your *Grammar Step by Step* book from the menu, and download the audio files.

To navigate the MP3 files, search for your: Lesson Number > Page Number > Activity Number.

Carolyn Graham's famous Grammar Chants are included in the full audio download for *Grammar Step by Step* and, for easy access, are also available to download separately. These chants infuse memorable rhythms with practical learning. Before long, students will feel the natural intonations and cadence of English, singing along to songs that are both instructive and fun!

Table of Contents

To the Teacher

Dear Colleagues,

As you know, our students are faced with all sorts of language input, and they depend on us to help them sort out the information that comes their way at school, at work, and in their daily lives. In the *Grammar Step by Step series,* we have divided grammatical information into digestible chunks that students can understand, and then provided practice in exercises that also help develop listening, speaking, reading, vocabulary, and writing skills.

With Book 2, we have zeroed in on ways to teach grammar clearly and systematically, and to isolate common areas of confusion in the beginning grammar class. We help students distinguish between, for example, the possessive, the contracted, and the plural *s.* And while we teach grammar, we teach lexical chunks of language associated with a theme or grammar point. For example, as students work on using the present tense for routine activities, they learn phrases used with *do, have, make* and *take.*

With over seventy-five years of English language teaching experience among us, we have worked to create material that not only goes step by step, but also engages students with contexts that they can relate to, and on occasion, be entertained by. Our contexts are varied, and the characters we portray reflect a wide range of backgrounds and ages. While the vocabulary we use is controlled so as not to distract from the grammar being studied, we have made an effort to use common and natural language that is essential for communication.

As our students work to learn English, we strive to keep them motivated, involved and rewarded, and to provide them with material that helps make sense of the chaos of language. We sincerely hope that with *Grammar Step by Step,* your students will find some order in the chaos, and have some fun at the same time.

Helen Kalkstein Fragiadakis   *Ellen Rosenfield*   *Carolyn Graham*

Overview of *Grammar Step by Step*

Grammar Step by Step 2 is the second in a three-level series of beginning to high intermediate books offering extensive grammar practice for young adult and adult learners. In *Grammar Step by Step*, small chunks of grammar are presented and practiced on a series of two-page spreads. While grammar presentation charts in many books present students with more new grammar than they can handle, the charts in *Grammar Step by Step* are designed to streamline the presentation of new grammar.

Each lesson in *Grammar Step by Step* features thorough practice of a grammar point, leading from controlled to open-ended activities. There are abundant opportunities for students to personalize learning through engaging speaking and writing tasks. Both lesser-trained and more experienced teachers will find the fresh and varied activity types meaningful and effective while enjoying the comfort of the accessible and predictable format.

Grammar Step by Step presents the content that experienced teachers expect to find in a grammar series, but also has a number of distinguishing features.

- **Flexible two-page lesson structure** allows teachers to select from a comprehensive array of lessons according to student and curricular needs.

- **Integrated skills approach to grammar** features initial listening activities that establish the grammar focus for reading, writing, and speaking tasks.

- **Carolyn Graham's chants** focus student attention on the oral/aural dimension of grammar learning while making classes lively and motivating.

- **Classroom-tested grammar points** target classic trouble spots like accurately using *have / do / make / take*.

- **Engaging illustrations** in each lesson visually define key vocabulary, allowing teachers and students to focus on grammar learning.

- **Resource-rich Teacher's Manual** reduces teacher prep time with reproducible tests and 64 expansion activities—one for each two-page lesson.

Components

The complete *Grammar Step by Step 2* program includes the following components:

- Student Book
- Teacher's Manual with answer key, 64 reproducible expansion activities, and a review test for each group of lessons
- Audiocassette/audio CD with recordings of all listening scripts and all chants, featuring Carolyn Graham

Guide to *Grammar Step by Step*

Each streamlined two-page lesson follows a **predictable and accessible format**.

Clear and concise charts introduce grammar points in easily comprehensible chunks.

Classroom-tested grammar points target classic trouble spots like accurately using the verb *go*.

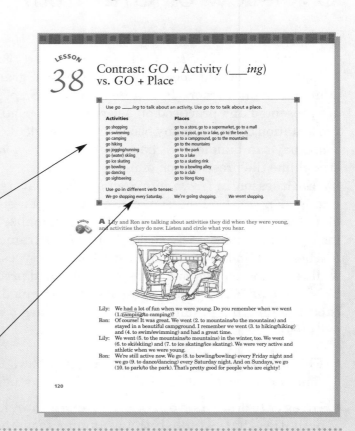

Engaging art illustrates **contexts** and teaches **new vocabulary words**.

One lesson in each group ends with a **chant** which allows students to practice the **pronunciation, rhythm, and intonation** of the new grammar point.

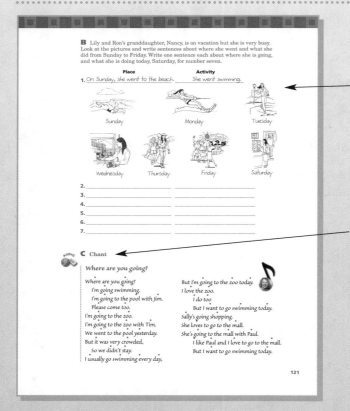

Margin notes alert students to relevant information provided elsewhere in the text.

The opening activity of each lesson acquaints students with the grammar point through a **context-building listening activity**.

Audio cassettes and audio CDs contain at least one listening activity per lesson, as well as 34 original chants written and recorded by Carolyn Graham.

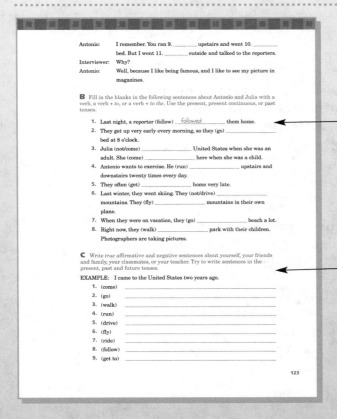

Tightly controlled exercises at the start of each lesson allow students to focus on the structure of the new grammar point.

Open-ended activities or chants at the close of each lesson provide students with opportunities to personalize the grammar point or interact with the grammar in an engaging way.

LESSON

39 Verbs + Ø, *to*, or *to the* + Places

"See appendix A for the Past tense forms of irregular verbs.

You can use certain verbs to talk about places.

come (back)	fly	go (back)	ride	walk
drive	follow somebody	get *	run	

* get to = arrive

These verbs can be followed by a place, to + a place, or to the + a place.

A Place	To + A Place	To the + A Place
here	to my house	to the doctor
there	to bed	to the store
inside	to school	to the park
outside	to work	to the zoo
upstairs	to church	to the beach
downstairs	to Miami (a city)	to the mall
uptown	to California (a state)	to the movies
downtown	to Canada (a country)	to the bank
home		to the mountains
everywhere		to the United States*
nowhere		* The United States is a country, but use 'the.'

Language Notes:
Use **come** when you are at the place you are talking about.
(the person speaking is at home): Can you come to my house tomorrow?
Use **go** when you are not at the place you are talking about.
(the person speaking is at home): Do you want to go to the movies tomorrow?

A Antonio and Julia are famous actors. They are giving an interview on TV. Fill in the blanks with *to, to the,* or Ø when nothing is necessary. Then listen and check your answers.

Interviewer: Do reporters and photographers follow you a lot?
Antonio: Yes, all the time. They follow us 1. _to the_ to the store, they follow us 2. _____ movies, they follow us 3. _____ home. They follow us 4. _____ everywhere.
Julia: Last month we took a trip. We went 5. _____ Spain. We went 6. _____ mountains and we went 7. _____ beach. But there were always people with cameras.
Interviewer: Did you ask them to go away?
Julia: Yes, but they didn't listen. And when we got 8. _____ home, there were reporters in front of our house. I cried.

122

Antonio: I remember. You ran 9. _____ upstairs and went 10. _____ bed. But I went 11. _____ outside and talked to the reporters.
Interviewer: Why?
Antonio: Well, because I like being famous, and I like to see my picture in magazines.

B Fill in the blanks in the following sentences about Antonio and Julia with a verb, a verb + *to,* or a verb + *to the.* Use the present, present continuous, or past tenses.

1. Last night, a reporter (follow) _followed_ them home.
2. They get up very early every morning, so they (go) _____ bed at 8 o'clock.
3. Julia (not/come) _____ United States when she was an adult. She (come) _____ here when she was a child.
4. Antonio wants to exercise. He (run) _____ upstairs and downstairs twenty times every day.
5. They often (get) _____ home very late.
6. Last winter, they went skiing. They (not/drive) _____ mountains. They (fly) _____ mountains in their own plane.
7. When they were on vacation, they (go) _____ beach a lot.
8. Right now, they (walk) _____ park with their children. Photographers are taking pictures.

C Write *true* affirmative and negative sentences about yourself, your friends and family, your classmates, or your teacher. Try to write sentences in the present, past and future tenses.

EXAMPLE: I came to the United States two years ago.

1. (come) _____
2. (go) _____
3. (walk) _____
4. (run) _____
5. (drive) _____
6. (fly) _____
7. (ride) _____
8. (follow) _____
9. (get to) _____

123

Each group of lessons is followed by a **two-page *Review*** in which students can test their recollection and understanding of the preceding grammar points.

Reviews begin with a **dictation** which incorporates both new grammar and new vocabulary from the previous lessons.

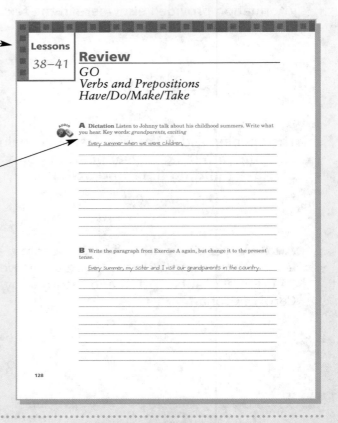

Lessons 38–41

Review
GO
Verbs and Prepositions
Have/Do/Make/Take

A **Dictation** Listen to Johnny talk about his childhood summers. Write what you hear. Key words: *grandparents, exciting*

Every summer when we were children,

B Write the paragraph from Exercise A again, but change it to the present tense.

Every summer, my sister and I visit our grandparents in the country.

128

C Look at the pictures of Diana and Johnny from Exercise A. Write about what they did when they visited their grandparents. Use the past tense.

They both:
• *went fishing with their grandfather.*
•

Diana:

Johnny:

D Correct the mistakes. Sentences 2 and 7 have two mistakes.
1. Johnny and Diana visited to their grandparents.
2. When they arrived to their grandparents house, they called to their parents.
3. Their grandparents took care them every summer.
4. Johnny listened music every day.
5. Diana told to her grandmother that she loved her.
6. The children talked their parents every Sunday.
7. They went to beach and went to swimming almost every day.
8. They didn't go school in July or August.
9. They went to home at the end of August.

129

Review activities ask students to **synthesize the grammar** that they've learned.

Error-correction activities allow students to identify and fix common errors that they might make themselves.

The **Have Fun activities** following each group of lessons reward students for their hard work.

Puzzles, **word games, and cooperative activities** allow students to use the new grammar in fun and entertaining ways.

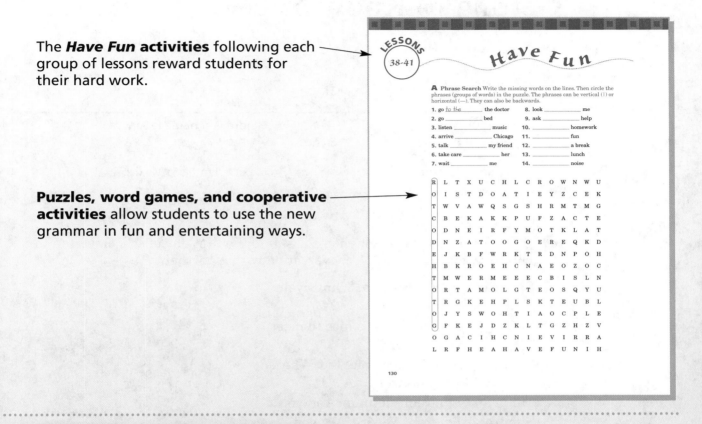

Many activities encourage students to use the new grammar to **interact with classmates**.

Each *Have Fun* spread closes with a lively **chant by Carolyn Graham**.

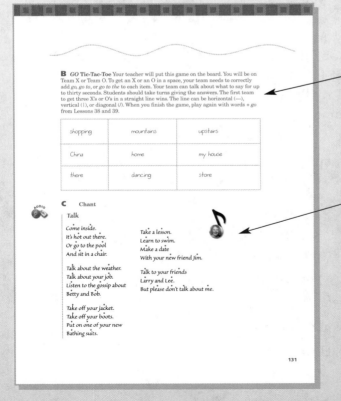

The **resource-rich Teacher's Manual** reduces teacher prep time with reproducible tests and 64 expansion activities—one for each two-page lesson!

Getting to Know You
The First Class

Questions	Answers
What's your name?	Sandra./My name is Sandra.
How do you spell it?	S-a-n-d-r-a.
How do you pronounce it?	Sán-dra.
Where are you from?	Mexico./I'm from Mexico.

A Sandra and Tan are in English class. It is the first day of school. Listen to the conversation. Practice the conversation with a partner.

Sandra: Hi. I'm Sandra. What's your name?

Tan: Hi. I'm Tan. It's nice to meet you, Sandra.

Sandra: Nice to meet you, too. Where are you from?

Tan: I'm from Vietnam. And you?

Sandra: I'm from Mexico. Are you a new student here?

Tan: Yes, it's my first day. And I'm a little nervous. How about you?

Sandra: I'm nervous, too. But I'm happy to be here because I really want to work on my grammar.

B **Walk and Talk** Walk around your classroom and have this conversation with at least five different students. Feel free to add questions and information. Speak, don't write.

A: Hi, I'm _____. What's your name?

B: Hi, I'm _____. It's nice to meet you, _____.

A: Nice to meet you, too. Where are you from?

B: I'm from _____. And you?

A: I'm from _____. Are you a new student here?

B: _____. How about you?

A: _____.

B: Well, it was nice talking to you. See you!

A: See you!

C Writing In a letter, introduce yourself to your classmates. You can write about any of the following: family, job, interests, or hobbies.

(date) ....

Dear Classmates,

I would like to tell you about myself. I ....

....

....

....

....

....

....

....

....

....

....

....

Here's to a good time together!

(name) ....

D Conversation Work with a partner or small group. Take turns reading your letters to each other. Your classmates will listen to you and then ask questions to get more details about you and your family.

After you finish your conversation, each student can tell the class one interesting thing about one other student. Say:

I would like to introduce .... _She / He_ ....

Introduction

Words to Know	
1. a partner	*(you, a partner — images)* *(a group — image)*
2. a group	
3. a question	What is your name?
4. an answer (a response)	My name is Ellen.
5. a sentence	My name is Ellen.
6. a paragraph	My name is Ellen. I am from Connecticut. Now I live in California. I am a teacher. I like teaching and writing books.
7. capital (upper case) letters	I am from **C**onnecticut.
8. small (lower case) letters	I **am from the** U.S.
9. vowels	Aa, Ee, Ii, Oo, Uu
10. consonants	Bb, Cc, Dd, Ff, Gg, Hh, Jj, Kk, Ll, Mm, Nn Pp, Qq, Rr, Ss, Tt, Vv, Ww, Xx, Yy, Zz

Directions	**Example**
1. Circle.	(teacher)
2. Underline.	<u>teacher</u>
3. Fill in the blank.	I am __from__ Connecticut.
4. Match.	__b__ 1. go to a. home __a__ 2. go b. Connecticut
5. Write the answer on the line.	A: Where are you from? B: __Connecticut__ .
6. Correct the grammar.	I am ~~come~~ from Connecticut. *I am from Connecticut.*
7. Complete the sentence.	Now I __live in California__.
8. Complete the chart.	Singular Plural book __books__ boy __boys__ __girl__ girls
9. Check the correct answer.	_____ This is a books. __√__ This is a book.

A Read the paragraph. Circle and correct the mistakes with capital and small letters. Work with a partner and compare your corrections.

I would like to tell you about myself and my family. i was born in the united states a long time ago. my family is very small. My parents are retired. My father was a Businessman and He was very busy. My Mother was a doctor and she was busy, too. they have a lot of free time now, so we can spend more time together. and I help them a lot Because they are getting older.

B **Word Search** Work with a partner and find the words in the puzzle. The words can be vertical (|), horizontal (—), or diagonal (/) (\). The words can also be spelled backwards.

capital	paragraph	vowel	consonant
underline	blank	~~grammar~~	sentence
partner	group	question	answer
check	circle	chart	match

```
C  T  H  P  A  R  A  G  R  A  P  H  M  A  R
A  N  T  S  R  W  B  J  E  C  A  O  V  Z  T
P  A  L  R  V  L  N  K  N  N  L  B  U  G  Q
I  N  H  T  A  H  M  G  I  O  C  A  A  W  D
T  O  M  G  E  H  R  M  L  I  N  H  J  K  R
A  S  N  I  S  A  C  R  R  T  F  M  E  B  E
L  N  X  Y  M  X  W  Y  E  S  R  N  Y  C  N
F  O  I  M  S  H  L  A  D  E  W  Q  R  O  K
V  C  A  E  C  B  S  D  N  U  U  E  N  E  R
S  R  L  T  I  L  D  R  U  Q  N  N  Q  N  B
M  H  A  T  R  A  R  B  N  T  I  T  N  V  T
Z  M  Q  C  U  N  G  R  R  I  V  O  W  E  L
P  L  P  I  M  K  A  A  H  U  G  R  O  U  P
E  L  C  R  I  C  P  R  E  W  S  N  A  Y  A
U  E  C  N  E  T  N  E  S  T  X  G  O  D  K
```

Nouns

Nouns are people, places, and things.

People		**Places**		**Things**	
Singular	**Plural**	**Singular**	**Plural**	**Singular**	**Plural**
a girl	girl<u>s</u>	an elevator	elevator<u>s</u>	a bed	bed<u>s</u>

Language Notes

A or *An* with Singular Nouns
- *A* and *an* = one. Use *a* and *an* with singular nouns.
- Use *a* when the noun starts with a consonant sound (a girl).
- Use *an* when the noun starts with a vowel sound (an <u>apple</u>).
- Don't use *a* and *an* with plural nouns (Incorrect: a girl<u>s</u>).

These words often come before nouns:

Before singular nouns: *a/an/the; one; my/your/his/her/our/their*
Before plural nouns: *the; two; three; my/your/his/her/our/their; some, many*
Examples: *the* student, *a* beautiful day, *his* cell phone; *two* students, *many* people

A It's the first day of school. Read the sentences. Circle the nouns. Then listen to check your answers.

1. There are many (people) in the class.

2. The room is very crowded.

3. Some students are waiting to talk to the teacher.

4. She is wearing a white sweater and black pants.

5. There are many things on her desk: a plant, some books, and an apple.

6. Two men are trying to fix the VCR.

7. Two students are writing in their notebooks.

B Put each noun from Exercise A in the correct column below. Include the words that come before the nouns (*some*, *the*, *three*, *his*, etc.).

Singular nouns	Plural nouns
the class	many people

> Nouns that are always plural:
> jeans
> pants
> shorts
> glasses

C Add two nouns to each list below. Use singular or plural forms. Then show your list to a classmate. Add your classmate's nouns to your list.

Clothes	People	Places Where People Work
a hat	friends	a supermarket
a dress	teachers	a school

D Look around your classroom. What people and things do you see? Write as many nouns as you can in three minutes. Use *a* or *an* before each singular noun.

a teacher, some women, two pencils

E Complete the following sentences with nouns. Share your sentences with a partner.

EXAMPLE: *There are* many desks *in this classroom.*

1. There are _____ in this classroom.

2. The teacher is wearing _____ .

3. There's _____ on my desk.

4. I see _____, _____,

   and _____ .

Adjectives

Adjectives are words that describe nouns.

Adjectives describe people: Maria is **homesick**.
Adjectives describe places: It's a **small** apartment.
Adjectives describe things: I miss your **delicious** dinners.

- **Adjectives come *before* nouns.**

Correct	Incorrect
It's a quiet street.	It's a ~~street quiet.~~

- **Adjectives come *after* the verb *BE* (*am, is, are*).**

Correct	Incorrect
I'm homesick.	~~I homesick.~~

- **Adjectives have *no* plural form.**

Correct	Incorrect
Clothes are expensive.	Clothes are ~~expensives.~~

- **Use *a* or *an* when the adjective comes before a singular noun.**
  Don't use *a* or *an* when the adjective is alone.

Correct	Incorrect
He is a handsome man.	~~He is handsome man.~~
He is handsome.	~~He is a handsome.~~

Common adjectives:

beautiful-ugly	expensive-cheap	comfortable-uncomfortable
big-small	new-old	married-single-divorced
cold-warm-hot	quiet-noisy	friendly-unfriendly
dangerous-safe	young-old	good-bad

A Read Maria's email to her mother. Circle the adjectives. Then listen to check your answers.

From: maria@mystuff.com   To: mom@mystuff.com
Subject: my new apartment   Sent: 9/4/06 8:02 p.m.

Hi Mom,

 I'm in my (new) apartment. It's small, but it's comfortable. It has a beautiful view from the bedroom, and it's on a quiet, safe street. I'm lucky that I found this apartment. The students in my class are friendly, but I'm still homesick. And I don't like the food here. I miss your delicious dinners. Also, the weather is very cold. I need to buy a warm coat, but clothes are expensive here.

 Oh! My favorite show is on TV now. I have to go. Bye!

Love, Maria

B Put each adjective from Exercise A in the correct column below. In the first column, include the nouns.

Before a noun	After the verb *BE*
new apartment	small

C Find the mistakes. Correct the sentences.

1. I have a house big.   I have a big house.
2. He is quiet boy.
3. The students are intelligents.
4. I have some books olds.
5. The food delicious.
6. I live on a street quiet.
7. My brother is a handsome.

D Complete the chart. What adjectives can describe these nouns? First, write what YOU think. Then work with a partner and share your answers.

Noun	You	Your Partner
a house	a beautiful house	an old house
a city		
a baby		
a friend		
an apple		
a book		
a movie		

LESSON

3 Verbs

Verbs are words that can show actions.

He **plays** soccer.　　　　I **eat** breakfast.

Some verbs do not show actions.

I **am** a student.　　　　They **like** cookies.

Verbs are often two words: a helping verb and a main verb.

	Helping Verb	Main Verb
It **is raining** today.	is	raining
He **doesn't eat** breakfast.	doesn't	eat
Do you **have** a job?	do	have

Verbs have affirmative, negative, and question forms:

Jose **works**.　　　　Jose **doesn't work**.　　　　**Does** Jose **work**?

Verbs have different tenses.

Present Tense:	Jose **works** every day.
Present Continuous Tense:	Jose **is working** now.
Past Tense:	Jose **worked** yesterday.
Future Tense:	Jose **is going to work** tomorrow.

A Complete the sentences with the verbs in the box. Use the verb *is* two times. Then listen to check your answers.

| eats | goes | misses | ~~rings~~ | watches |
| gets | is | plays | takes | works |

Jose's alarm clock ___*rings*___ every day at 5:00 a.m. He _____

up and _____ breakfast. Then he _____ the bus to work.

He _____ all day. After work, he _____ soccer with his

friends. At night, he _____ very tired. He _____ TV and

then _____ to bed. He _____ far away from his family. He

_____ his family very much.

10

B Circle the verbs. Write each verb in the correct column. If there is no helping verb, write Ø.

	Helping Verb	Main Verb
1. I'm (studying) English.	'm	studying
2. I came here last year.	Ø	came
3. It's raining today.		
4. We don't have class tomorrow.		
5. Are you homesick?		
6. I miss my family.		
7. Do you have a job?		
8. We are tired.		

C Check (✔) *main verb* or *adjective* for each underlined word.

	Main Verb	Adjective
1. He <u>plays</u> soccer.	✓	
2. He's a <u>new</u> student.		
3. I <u>need</u> a new coat.		
4. I'm very <u>busy</u>.		
5. Are you <u>married</u>?		
6. Do you <u>want</u> to stay home?		
7. What time does the class <u>begin</u>?		
8. I'm not <u>hungry</u>.		

D Chant

Sleepy Woman

Her alarm clock rings at six o'clock,
But she stays in bed until seven.
She gets up, she takes a shower,
Then she goes back to bed until eleven.

At eleven o'clock she gets up again.
Her cat sits on her lap.
She feeds her cat, she has an early lunch,
Then she goes back to bed for a nap.

LESSON 4 Prepositions

Some prepositions show place or time.

Place	Time
We're **in** New York.	The school year starts **in** September.
It's **on** Main Street.	Classes begin **on** Monday.
The tour begins **at** the bookstore.	My class is **at** 8:00 a.m.
in a city, country, continent (**in** Peru)	**in** a month, year (**in** June, in 2001)
on a street, floor, (on the second floor)	**on** a day (**on** Tuesday, **on** my birthday)
at a store, school, home (at the bookstore)	**at** a time (at 8:30, at midnight)

Some prepositions follow certain words.

welcome **to**   register **for**
come **from**   the end **of** (the class, the day)
go **to**   walk **to**

Some common prepositions include:

after	behind	in	on
at	for	of	to*
before	from	near	with

*to in front of a verb is not a preposition. It is part of an infinitive: **to be, to eat**

A phrase is a group of words. A prepositional phrase starts with a preposition and ends with a noun.

> *See Appendix I for prepositions of time and place.*
>
> *See Appendix J for phrases with prepositions.*

 A Mark is giving a tour of Milton College to some new students. Listen to the beginning of the tour. Write the preposition you hear.

Good afternoon. My name is Mark. Welcome ___to___ Milton College. Our tour begins _____ the campus bookstore. You can buy books, school supplies, and even toothpaste _____ the store. We'll come back here at the end _____ the tour.

First, we'll walk _____ the art building. You'll see some examples of student art _____ the second floor. Then we'll go _____ the administration building. This is a busy time for us. The fall semester begins _____ Wednesday, so right now many students are registering _____ their classes. Our students come _____ all over the world. I'll give you a chance to talk to them _____ the tour.

B Write the correct preposition (*at, in, from, of, on, to*) in each sentence. Then circle each prepositional phrase.

1. Classes begin .... ⟨on............ Tuesday.⟩

2. My first class is .... 10:30 a.m.

3. I usually walk .... school.

4. I come .... a small city.

5. My house is .... Center Street.

6. My apartment is .... the second floor.

7. I go .... school every day.

8. My parents live .... South America.

9. I was born .... 1990.

10. This is the end .... this exercise.

C David is a new student at Milton College. Read his letter to his cousin in Peru. Underline the prepositions.

> Dear Alex,
>
>   It's 2:00 <u>in</u> the afternoon. I am at a small college in New York called Milton College. I am in the main office of the college. The office is on the first floor in room 22.
>
>   Many students are standing in line. The secretary is very busy. There are a lot of papers on her desk. There is a sign on the wall. The sign says, "Classes begin on Wednesday, September 4."
>
>   My first class is on Wednesday at 9:00. I am very excited.
>
>   Your cousin,
>   David

D Read the paragraph about David. Circle the prepositions. Then write a paragraph about yourself and share it with a partner.

   I'm ⟨from⟩ Peru. I live in the U.S. with my family. Right now I am at school. My school is on Eighth Avenue in New York. My class is in room 26 on the first floor. My class is on Monday and Wednesday from 9:00 a.m. to 11:00 a.m.

   I'm from .... I live in ....

....

....

....

....

Sentences

A sentence has a subject and a verb.

Subject	Verb	
I	paint	bridges.
My name	is	Imelda.
This	is	my dog Jake.

The subject of a sentence is a noun or a subject pronoun. It is usually the first noun or subject pronoun in the sentence. It often tells who or what is doing the action.

Subject Pronouns:	Singular	Plural
	I	we
	you	you
	he, she, it	they

Don't use a noun and a subject pronoun together.

Correct	Incorrect
My parents work in a factory.	~~My parents they work in a factory.~~
They work in a factory.	

A Listen to a TV show about unusual jobs. Draw lines to match the subjects and the verbs.

Subject	Verb
1. Fran Fido	a. <u>walks</u> dogs.
2. Bart Highsmith	b. <u>shops</u> for people.
3. Mark Magnum	c. <u>paints</u> bridges.
4. Mel Minton	d. <u>have</u> unusual jobs.
5. Many people	e. <u>trains</u> lions.

B Find the subjects and the verbs in the sentences. Write them on the lines.

		Subject	Verb
1.	Many people have unusual jobs.	people	have
2.	Bart Highsmith paints bridges.		
3.	This is Fran.		
4.	She walks dogs for money.		
5.	It isn't very hard work.		
6.	Mel shops for people.		
7.	Some people don't have time.		
8.	Mel doesn't make a lot of money.		

C Find the mistakes. Put a check (✔) under the type of mistake you find for each item.

		No Subject	No Verb	Noun + Subject Pronoun
1.	Is difficult.	✔		
2.	His job dangerous.			
3.	Works hard.			
4.	Imelda she has an easy job.			
5.	This not hard work.			
6.	Her life it's difficult.			
7.	They like the U.S., but is expensive.			

D Find two classmates with jobs. Ask them the questions below and write their answers in the chart.

Name	What is your job?	Is your job dangerous?	Is your job easy?	Do you like your job?
Chan	plumber	yes	no	yes
1.				
2.				

Write a paragraph about one classmate. Label the subject (s) and the verb (v) in your sentences.

EXAMPLE:

s   v   s v   s   v   s v   s   v
Chan has a job. He's a plumber. His job is dangerous. It's not easy, but he likes it.

Review
Parts of Speech and Sentences

A **Dictation** Listen to the paragraph about Lisa's family. Write what you hear. Then circle the subjects and underline the verbs. Key words: *daughter, husband*

My (name) is Lisa.

B Look at the photo of Lisa's family at a park.

Part 1: What people and things do you see in the picture? Write eight more nouns below. Use your dictionary. Write *a*, *an*, or a number (*two, three, four*) before each noun.

1. six plates
2. a woman
3.
4.
5.

6.
7.
8.
9.
10.

Part 2: Choose five nouns from your list in Part 1. Write *a, an,* or a number and the adjective + noun.

	a/an/a number	adjective + noun
1.	six	big plates
2.		
3.		
4.		
5.		

Part 3: What actions do you see in the picture? Write four more verbs below.

1.	cook	**4.**	
2.	fly	**5.**	
3.		**6.**	

C Read about the picture in Exercise B. Underline the prepositional phrases.

It's a beautiful day. Many people are <u>in the park</u>. Birds are flying in the sky. The sun is shining. Lisa's family is having a picnic under a beautiful tree. Lisa is putting fruit in a big bowl. Her husband is cooking hamburgers on the grill. David is throwing a ball to his brother. Lisa's father is sleeping on a comfortable chair. Everyone is having a good time.

D Look at each underlined word. Check (✔) noun, pronoun, main verb, or adjective.

		Noun	Pronoun	Main Verb	Adjective
1.	<u>It</u>'s a sunny day.		✔		
2.	The <u>wind</u> is blowing.				
3.	Birds are flying in the <u>sky</u>.				
4.	His brother isn't <u>married</u>.				
5.	They don't <u>have</u> children.				
6.	The hamburgers are <u>ready</u>.				
7.	The baby is <u>crying</u>.				
8.	She's holding her <u>favorite</u> doll.				
9.	She <u>wants</u> some candy.				
10.	<u>They</u>'re having fun.				
11.	Many people love the <u>park</u>.				
12.	<u>It</u> closes at 10:00 p.m.				

Have Fun

A **Word Search** Write *noun, adjective,* or *verb* next to each word below. Then find and circle each word in the puzzle. The words can be vertical (|), horizontal (—), or diagonal (/) (\). The words can also be spelled backwards.

1. begin *verb*
2. dangerous
3. does
4. eats
5. favorite

6. friendly
7. handsome
8. morning
9. museum
10. noisy

11. people
12. sweater
13. want
14. wears
15. weather
16. write

```
F Y N Y H G E W D P M I
W B S W L P R A C E U C
H E H I E D N A T G S H
S L A O O G N I M G E A
R E P T E N R E N X U N
A L A R H W S I I X M D
E N O T N E N T K R M S
W U W R S R R M V O F O
S M A D O (B E G I N) V M
B W N M S W E A T E R E
N F T D O E S K I S C O
F A V O R I T E Y C U L
```

B Write any noun, verb, or adjective, on the lines.

1. Write an adjective. _busy_

2. Write an action verb. ....

3. Write an action verb. ....

4. Write a plural noun (thing). ....

5. Write a singular noun (place). ....

6. Write an action verb. ....

7. Write an adjective. ....

C Fill in the blanks with the words from Exercise B. Then read your story.

I'm a very (1)................ person. I (2)................ all day and (3)................
all night. I have many (4)................ in my (5)................, but they
(6)................ too much! I hope that some day I will be very (7)................ .

D Chant

Families

He has an interesting job, a beautiful wife,
Two smart daughters, and a comfortable life.

She has a handsome husband, an exciting job,
And an old, intelligent dog named Bob.

They have a very big family in a very small house,
A lazy cat, and a hardworking mouse.

We have a new bike and an old car,
An expensive piano and a good guitar.

LESSON 6

BE—Affirmative and Negative Statements

BE in the present tense has three forms: *am, is, are*.

Affirmative		Negative	
Full Forms	**Contractions**	**Full Forms**	**Contractions**
I am	I'm	I am not	I'm not
You are	You're	You are not	You're not *OR* You aren't
He is	He's	He is not	He's not *OR* He isn't
She is	She's	She is not	She's not *OR* She isn't
It is	It's	It is not	It's not *OR* It isn't
We are	We're	We are not	We're not *OR* We aren't
They are	They're	They are not	They're not *OR* They aren't

Use *BE* with adjectives, nouns, and places.

with adjectives:	The food is delicious.
with nouns:	I'm not a doctor.
with places:	We're from Hong Kong.

Use *am/is/are* to talk about age:

Correct: I'm twenty years old.

Incorrect: ~~I have twenty years old.~~

 A Julie's neighborhood is having a block party. Julie is talking to Mark. Read the sentences. Then listen and circle *T* for *True* or *F* for *False*.

1. The food is delicious.   T   F
2. The weather is beautiful.   T   F
3. Mark and his family are from Hong Kong.   T   F
4. The traffic is terrible in Hong Kong.   T   F
5. Life in Hong Kong is not expensive.   T   F
6. Mark is a doctor.   T   F
7. Mark's children are with him.   T   F
8. Julie's son is 15 years old.   T   F

B Complete the chart.

Affirmative	Negative 1	Negative 2
1. It's boring.	It's not boring.	It isn't boring.
2.	He's not a doctor.	
3.		They aren't from Korea.
4. He's at home.		
5.	She's not 15 years old.	
6.		It isn't cloudy.

C Complete these sentences to make *true* sentences. Use the negative and affirmative forms of *BE*. Use contractions when possible.

1. I _____'m not_____ a teacher.
2. I _____ a student.
3. We _____ in Hong Kong.
4. The food in this country _____ delicious.
5. The students in this class _____ friendly.
6. The traffic here _____ terrible.
7. My classmates and I _____ on vacation now.
8. I _____ married.

D Find the mistakes. Correct the sentences.

1. Is a beautiful day.   _It's a beautiful day._
2. I married.   _____
3. You in this class.   _____
4. He no hungry.   _____
5. I like this food. Is delicious. _____
6. My children are'nt on vacation. _____
7. Some students is homesick.   _____
8. He has fifteen years old.   _____

BE—Yes-No Questions and Short Answers

Statement:	You	are	late.

Yes/No Question: Are you late?
Short Answers: Yes, I am.   No, I'm not.

Yes-No Questions	Short Answers		
	Affirmative (No Contraction)	**Negative** (Contraction OK)	
Am I late?	Yes, you are.	No, you're not. *OR* No, you aren't.	
Are you tired?	Yes, I am.	No, I'm not.	
Is your daughter in bed?	Yes, she is.	No, she's not. *OR* No, she isn't.	
Is it cold?	Yes, it is.	No, it's not. *OR* No, it isn't.	
Is he in the lobby?	Yes, he is.	No, he's not. *OR* No, he isn't.	
Are we at the hotel?	Yes, you are.	No, you're not. *OR* No, you aren't.	
Are they comfortable?	Yes, they are.	No, they're not. *OR* No, they aren't.	

A Jake and his family are on vacation in California. Jake is talking to his mother on the phone. Listen and write *is* or *are*.

Mom: Hi, Jake.

Jake: Hi, Mom.

Mom: .... you tired? .... you in bed?

Jake: Mom! It's 5:00 a.m. here in California!

Mom: Oh, I'm sorry. How are all of you? .... the kids OK?

Jake: We're all fine, Mom!

Mom: How is the weather? .... it cold out?

Jake: No, it's very nice.

Mom: And how is the hotel? .... the beds comfortable? .... the food good?

Jake: Everything is wonderful.

Mom: How about the rooms? .... the rooms noisy?

Jake: No, they're not. They're fine. Can I talk to you later, Mom?

Mom: Oh, I'm sorry. You're tired. But one more question. .... the hotel expensive?

Jake: Well, it's a little expensive, but it's really nice.

B Jake and his family are having dinner at Mandy's restaurant. Put the words in the correct order to make yes-no questions. Then write short answers with pronouns.

1. in/Maya and Jake/New York/are

   Question: _Are Maya and Jake in New York?_   Answer: _No, they aren't._

2. Jake/on vacation/is

   Question: _____   Answer: _Yes,_

3. rainy/it/a/day/is

   Question: _____   Answer: _No,_

4. very/Mandy's/is/a/restaurant/famous

   Question: _____   Answer: _Yes,_

5. full/the restaurant/is/of people

   Question: _____   Answer: _Yes,_

6. baby/in Maya's lap/is/the

   Question: _____   Answer: _No,_

C Find the mistakes. Rewrite the questions.

1. Is expensive the hotel?   _Is the hotel expensive?_

2. Is crowded the restaurant?   _____

3. Is noisy?   _____

4. Jake is hungry now?   _____

5. Is cold in California?   _____

6. Is the people at home?   _____

D Chant

Guessing game

Am I late?
  Yes you are. You're *very* late.
  It's *eight* o'clock.

It's *not* eight.
  Yes, it is.
No, it's not.
  Yes, it is.

I'm *not* late.
  Yes, you are.
  You're late. You're late.
  It's a quarter to eight.

I'm not late.
  Your watch is slow.
  It's eight o'clock.
  You're late. You're late.

When, Where, What, Who Questions with *BE*

Wh- word	BE	Subject	Short Answer
When	is	your birthday?	September 20.
Where	are	you from?	New York.
What	is	your favorite color?	Red.
Who	is	your best friend?	Tina.
When	are	your classes?	In the morning.

WHAT + noun	BE	Subject	Short Answer
What color	are	her eyes?	Blue.
What time	is	it?	3:00 a.m.
What city	are	you from?	New York.
What nationality	are	you?	Brazilian.

A Tom and Laura are on a TV game show called "The Marriage Game." The game is for husbands and wives. Complete the *Wh* questions. Then listen and match the questions and answers.

_f_ **1.** When _is_____ her birthday?   **a.** Tina.

____ **2.** What _____ Laura's favorite color?   **b.** Green.

____ **3.** Where _____ she from?   **c.** Red.

____ **4.** What nationality _____ her parents?   **d.** Brazilian.

____ **5.** What color _____ her eyes?   **e.** Today.

____ **6.** Who _____ her best friend?   **f.** September 20.

____ **7.** When _____ Tom and Laura's   **g.** New York.
wedding anniversary?

B Laura got all the answers right. Write *Wh* questions for her answers.

1. Game Show Host: _What is his favorite sport?_____

Laura: His favorite sport is soccer.

2. Game Show Host: _____

Laura: His favorite movie is Star Wars.

3. Game Show Host: _____

Laura: His eyes are brown.

4. Game Show Host: _____

Laura: He's from Los Angeles.

5. Game Show Host: _____

Laura: His birthday is on March 22.

6. Game Show Host: _____

Laura: His best friend's name is Harry.

C Complete the questions with the words in the box. Then practice with a partner.

city	country	month	time
color	day	nationality	year

1. A: What ____color____ are your eyes?   B: They're brown.

2. A: What _____ is it today?   B: It's Wednesday.

3. A: What _____ is it now?   B: It's 10:30 a.m.

4. A: What _____ are you from?   B: I'm from France.

5. A: What _____ are you from?   B: I'm from Paris.

6. A: What _____ is your birthday?   B: June.

7. A: What _____ is your car?   B: 1999.

8. A: What _____ are you?   B: I'm French.

D Complete the questions below. Then ask three students to answer the questions. Write their answers in the chart.

NAME	Where _____ are you from?	_____ is your birthday?	_____ is your favorite movie?	_____ is your favorite actor?
José	Mexico City, Mexico.	November 9.	Lord of the Rings.	Brad Pitt.

Review

BE with Affirmative and Negative Statements, Yes-No Questions, *Wh* Questions

 A **Dictation** It is December in New York. Bob meets Marie at a coffee shop. Listen to their conversation. Write what you hear. Key words: *vacation*, *Peru*

Bob: Hi, are you _____

Marie: _____

_____

Bob: _____

Marie: _____

Bob: _____

_____

Marie: _____

_____

B Continue the conversation in the coffee shop. Add the missing parts of the conversation.

Bob: Oh, by the way… My name _____is_____ Bob. _____ your name?

Marie: I _____ Marie. It's nice to meet you.

Bob: It's nice to meet you, too. _____ this your first trip to New York?

Marie: No, it _____. I was here three years ago. I studied English here.

Bob: Your English _____ very good!

Marie: Thank you! _____ you a student in New York?

Bob: No, I _____. I'm a lawyer. My office is around the corner.

Marie: Uh-oh! What time _____?

Bob: _____ 4:00 p.m.

Marie: Oh, I'm late. It was nice meeting you.

Bob: It was nice talking to you. Enjoy your vacation!

C Read Marie's email to her friend Linda. Circle the adjectives and underline the prepositional phrases. Then write the paragraph again on the lines below. Change *I* to *she*. Change *we* to *they*. Change *my* to *her*.

> Hi Linda,
>
> I'm not <u>at home</u> right now. I'm on vacation with my parents. We're in New York. I'm in my room at a (beautiful) hotel. I'm awake but my parents are in bed. We're very lucky because the weather is beautiful. New York is fun and exciting. I'm not ready to go back to Peru.
> See you soon!
> Marie

Marie isn't at home right now. She's _____

_____

_____

_____

_____

_____

D Complete the chart.

Affirmative	Negative (two ways)	Yes-No Question	*Wh* Question
She is from France.	She isn't from France. She's not from France.	Is she from France?	Where is she from?
The party is on Saturday.	It		When
My parents are at the hotel.	They		Where

Have Fun

A Crossword Puzzle

Across

2. I have two children, a .... and a daughter.

3. My birthday is .... September 20.

4. A: What .... are you from?
B: I'm from Beijing.

6. Where is he ....?

8. A: .... are my keys?
B: They're on the table.

9. A: Are you married?
B: No I'm ....

Down

1. My birthday is .... November.

2. My favorite .... is soccer.

4. A: What .... are your eyes?
B: They're brown.

5. The American flag is red, white, and ....

6. A: Are you .... tomorrow?
B: No, I'm busy.

7. A: .... is Thanksgiving?
B: It's in November.

8. .... time is it?

B Chant

Guessing Game

His hair is brown,
It isn't gray.
He isn't from Dallas,
He's from San Jose.

When's his birthday?
    The first of May.
    What's his name?
His name is Ray.

Her hair is white,
Her eyes are blue.
Her grandson, Tim, is twenty-two.

    Is she from Brooklyn?
Yes, she is.
What's her name?
    Her name is Liz.

San Jose is a large city near San Francisco, California.

Brooklyn is one of the sections of New York City.

How Questions with *BE*

	Questions			Answers		
How	**BE**	**Subject**	**Subject**	**BE**	**Adjective**	
How	are	you?	I	am	fine.	
How	is	the soup?	It	is	delicious.	
How	are	the children?	They	are	great!	
How	is	the weather?	It	is	cold.	

Contraction: How is = How's

How + Adjective	**BE**	**Subject**	**Subject**	**BE**	
How old	are	you?	I	am	58.
How tall	is	he?	He	is	5 feet tall.
How much	is	it?	It	is	$10.00.
How far	is	it from here?	It	is	two blocks away.

A Elsa and Lena are at a restaurant. Read the conversation. Underline the questions with *how*. Circle the subject and the verb *BE* in each question. Then listen to the conversation.

Elsa: How is your salad?
Lena: Wonderful. How's your soup?
Elsa: It's delicious. So Lena, how's your son? How's his new job?
Lena: He's fine, but his new job is very difficult.
Elsa: And how's your grandson?
Lena: He's great. Here's a picture of him.
Elsa: He's tall now! How tall is he?
Lena: He's almost 6 feet tall.
Elsa: Wow! And how old is he now?
Lena: He's 16 years old. He's in his junior year of high school.
Waiter: Excuse me. Here's the check. I hope you enjoyed your lunch.
Lena: Yes, we did. Thank you.
Elsa: How much is it?
Lena: It's only $20.00. But it's my treat.
Elsa: No, no…Please…I want to pay.
Lena: No, no, no…You treated me last time.
Elsa: Well, OK. Thank you, Lena.

B Complete each of Lena's questions. Use *How / How much / How tall / How old / How far + is / are*.

1. Lena: _____How's_____ your daughter-in-law?

   Elsa: She's fine.

2. Lena: _____ her parents?

   Elsa: Her father is fine, but her mother isn't doing well. She's in the hospital.

3. Lena: That's too bad. _____ she?

   Elsa: I'm not sure, but I think she's in her nineties!

4. Lena: Wow! And _____ your son, Ron?

   Elsa: He's doing very well. He's buying a house!

5. Lena: That's wonderful! _____ houses in his area?

   Elsa: They're very expensive.

6. Lena: _____ his new house from his job?

   Elsa: It's not very far. It's only one mile from his office.

7. Lena: That's great! _____ his children?

   Elsa: They're fine.

C Add two more questions to the list below. Then ask three classmates about their favorite restaurants. Write your classmates' answers on the right.

Questions	Answers
1. What's your favorite restaurant?	....
2. How far is it from here?	....
3. How is the service?	....
4. How are the prices?	....
5.	....
6.	....

D Chant

So Many Questions

Mary's very young.
   How old is she?
She's seventeen, but she looks twenty–three.
Bob's very tall.
   How tall is he?
I think he's over six foot three.
He's not in New York.
   Where is he?

He's living near the White House,
                in Washington, D.C.
   How's his apartment?
He likes it a lot.
      How's the weather in the summer?
It's very, very hot.

Statements and Questions with *There is* and *There are*

Affirmative Statement	**There**	**is/are**	**Subject**	**Prepositional Phrase**
	There	is	a TV	in the living room.
	There	are	two bedrooms	in the apartment.
	Contraction: *There is = There's*			
Negative Statement	**There**	**is/are + not**	**Subject**	**Prepositional Phrase**
	There	isn't	an elevator	in the building.
	There	aren't	*any stores	near the apartment.
	*Use *any* in negative statements with plural subjects.			
Yes-No Question	**Is/Are**	**There**	**Subject**	**Prepositional Phrase**
	Is	there	an elevator	in the building?
	Are	there	two bathrooms	in the apartment?
	Are	there	*any children	in the neighborhood?
	*Use *any* in questions.			
	Short Answers: Yes, there is. No, there isn't.			
	Yes, there are. No, there aren't.			

A Dan is talking to his older sister about his new apartment. Complete the questions with *Is there* or *Are there*. Then listen to the conversation and write short answers.

	Questions	Answers
1.	*Are there* any supermarkets nearby?	*No, there aren't.*
2.	.... two bedrooms?	....
3.	.... two bathrooms?	....
4.	.... a bathtub?	....
5.	.... a dining room?	....
6.	.... a dishwasher?	....
7.	.... an elevator?	....

B Look at the picture of Dan's bedroom in Exercise A. Complete the sentences below. Use *There's, There isn't, There are,* or *There aren't*. Use *any* in negative statements with plural subjects.

1. _____There's_____ a bed in the bedroom.
2. _____ a desk.
3. _____ a clock.
4. _____ chairs.
5. _____ CDs on the bed.
6. _____ boxes on the floor.
7. _____ a cat on the bed.

C Complete the questions about your house and your neighborhood. Use *Is there* or *Are there*. Write *true* short answers.

	Questions	Answers
1.	_____Is there_____ a shower in your apartment?	_____
2.	_____ a bathtub in your house?	_____
3.	_____ a garage in your building?	_____
4.	_____ children in your neighborhood?	_____
5.	_____ a park near your house?	_____
6.	_____ many stores in your neighborhood?	_____
7.	_____ people from many countries in your neighborhood?	_____

D Talk to a classmate. Ask him or her three questions from Exercise C. Then write sentences about your classmate.

EXAMPLE: There is a garage in Maria's building. There aren't any children in her neighborhood. There are many stores in her neighborhood.

_____

_____

_____

_____

_____

LESSON 11

Contrast: Subject Pronouns and Possessive Adjectives

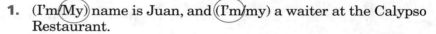

Subject Pronoun + *BE*
I am/I'm a waiter.
You are/You're late.
He is/He's an accountant.
She is/She's a doctor.
It is/It's near Brazil.
We are/We're late.
They are/They're married.

Possessive Adjective + Noun
My name is Juan.
Your teacher is in room 202.
His name is Juan.
Her name is Veronica.
Its capital is Montevideo.
Our teacher is late.
Their son is 10 years old.

Pronunciation Notes
It's and *its* sound the same.
You're and *your* sound the same.
They're and *their* sound the same. (*There* sounds like these words, too.)
He's and *his* DO NOT sound the same.

A Juan is telling his class about his family and his country. Circle the correct words in each sentence. Then listen to the sentences.

1. (I'm/**My**) name is Juan, and (**I'm**/my) a waiter at the Calypso Restaurant.

2. (I'm/My) from Uruguay. (It's/Its) a very small country in South America.

3. (It's/Its) south of Brazil.

4. (It's/Its) capital is Montevideo.

5. This is a picture of my brother. (He's/His) name is David.

6. (He's/His) thirty years old, and (he's/his) married.

7. He and (he's/his) wife both work in the U.S.

8. (They're/ Their) both accountants. (They're / Their) jobs are very difficult.

9. They have a son and a daughter. (They're/Their) daughter is a doctor. (She's/Her) name is Lucia.

10. (They're/Their) son is a university student. (He's/His) twenty-one years old.

11. (We're/Our) in the U.S., but (we're/our) parents are still in Uruguay.

34

B Circle each subject pronoun. Underline each possessive adjective.

1. His name is David.
2. He's married to Anita.
3. They are accountants.
4. Their daughter is here.
5. She is single.

6. Her brother isn't here.
7. He's 21.
8. They're nice people.
9. We're from Uruguay.
10. Our children are in school.

C Juan is showing some photos to his classmate Chan. Circle the correct word in each sentence.

Chan: Is that you? Are those (1. you're/your) parents?
Juan: Uh huh. I'm about five years old in that picture.
      (2. It's/Its) my birthday.
Chan: (3. You're/Your) very cute in this picture!
Juan: Thank you!
Chan: What city is this?
Juan: (4. It's/Its) the capital of Uruguay.
      (5. It's/Its) name is Montevideo.
Chan: (6. It's/Its) very beautiful.
Juan: Yes, but (7. it's/its) very crowded!
Chan: Who are the people in the photo?
Juan: My brother and his wife.
      (8. They're/Their) both accountants.
      (9. They're/Their) work is very difficult.
Chan: They look tired in this picture.
Juan: (10. They're/Their) always tired, especially at tax time!
Chan: Who's this?
Juan: That's my aunt. (11. She's/Her) name is Sandra.
      (12. She's/Her) married to a man from Chicago.
      (13. He's/His) name is Van. (14. He's/His) a famous pianist.

D Read the information about Chan. Then write about Chan. Change *I* to *he*, *we* to *they*, *my* to *his* and *our* to *their*. Look for verbs that need to be changed.

My name is Chan. I'm Chinese. I am in New York, but my parents are still in China. I'm a computer programmer. My job is very difficult, but it's very interesting. I'm married and my wife is a preschool teacher. We're both very busy. Our son is five years old. His name is Ping.

His name is Chan.

_____

_____

_____

_____

Now, write a paragraph about yourself on a separate piece of paper.

Review

How Is/How Are, There Is/There Are
Subject Pronouns vs. Possessive Adjectives

 A **Dictation** Listen to a person asking for directions. Write what you hear. Then practice the conversation with a partner. Key words: *pharmacy*, *Center Street*

A: Excuse me. ....

....

B: ....

....

A: ....

....

B: ....

....

B Fill in the blanks with possessive adjectives (my, his, her, its, your, our, their) or subject pronouns + BE (I'm, he's, she's, it's, you're, we're, they're).

1. My .... name is Mark. I love to brag. I'm .... very rich.

2. My parents have a big company. .... rich, too. ....
   company makes a lot of money.

3. My brother is a famous baseball player. .... the best player
   on the team. .... team always wins!

4. We have a vacation house. .... vacation house is on the
   ocean. .... a very beautiful house.

5. My sister always looks great. .... clothes are expensive.
   .... a beautiful woman.

6. My sons are good at sports. .... on the basketball team at
   school. .... team is the best.

C Read the paragraph about Mark's sons, David and Charles. Rewrite the paragraph, but this time write just about David.

These are my twin sons. They're thirteen years old. Their names are David and Charles. They're very cute. Their birthday is in June. They're very smart and very popular. When they aren't in school, they're with their friends at the mall.

This is my son. He ....

....

....

....

D Draw a picture of a friend or family member. Write a paragraph about the person. Use the paragraph in Exercise C as an example.

This is ....

....

....

....

....

....

....

....

....

....

E Find the mistakes. Rewrite the questions. Then write possible answers to the questions on a separate piece of paper.

1. How tall you are? How tall are you? ....

2. How old your brother? ....

3. What is he's name? ....

4. How is your friends? ....

5. What time are they classes? ....

6. Are they many people in your class? ....

7. Is there a lot of students from your country? ....

8. How is you're English? ....

Have Fun

A Crossword Puzzle

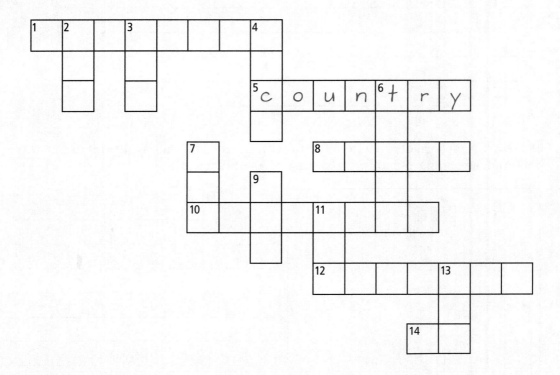

Across

1. There's no shower in the ....
5. Uruguay is a small ....
8. I have my book. The students have .... books.
10. I have two children, a son and a ....
12. A: How is the ....? B: It's sunny.
14. .... there a dishwasher in your apartment?

Down

2. How .... your children?
3. This is my mother. .... name is Carmen.
4. A: How .... is it? B: It's $20.
6. .... are many students in this class.
7. A: Today is my birthday. B: How .... are you?
9. We have a son and a daughter. .... son's name is Joe.
11. .... is your lunch? It's delicious.
13. This is my father. .... name is Sam.

B Chant

Good Student, Good Teacher

He's a student.
His name is Lee.
　　How old is he?
He's twenty-three.

She's a teacher.
Her name is Dee.
　　Where does she teach?
At USC.

　　How's her class?
Her class is great.
　　How are the students?
They're never late.

She's an excellent teacher.
Her students are fine.
I think her class
Is better than mine.

USC=University of
Southern California

Present Tense—Affirmative and Negative Statements

Use the present tense to talk about something that repeats or is routine.

Affirmative		Negative	
I/You/ We/They	work.	I/You/ We/ They	don't work.
He/She/It	works.	He/She/It	doesn't work.

Correct:	He works.	**Correct:**	He doesn't work.
Incorrect:	~~He work.~~	**Incorrect:**	~~He don't work. He doesn't works.~~

Spelling:
Use the base form of the verb with *I, you, we,* and *they*. With *he, she,* or *it*, follow these rules.

1. Add *s* to most verbs:	eat-eats	play-plays
2. Add **es** to verbs that end in *ch, sh, ss,* or *x*:	watch-watches	miss-misses
3. When a verb ends in consonant + *y*, drop the *y* and add *ies*:	study-studies	try-tries
4. Some verbs are irregular:	have-has do-does go-goes	

A Read about Javier and Ernesto. Circle the correct forms of the verbs in parentheses. Then listen to check your answers.

Javier and his uncle Ernesto (1. lives/<u>live</u>) in the same apartment. They both (2. comes/come) from Mexico. They (3. works/work) in the same expensive restaurant. But they (4. doesn't see/don't see) each other very much. Why not?

They (5. has/have) different work schedules. Javier (6. works/work) during the evening, but Ernesto (7. doesn't work /don't work) during the evening. He (8. goes/go) to work early in the morning and (9. go/goes) to sleep early.

Ernesto (10. has/have) the "graveyard shift." He (11. wakes up/wake up) at 3:00 a.m., (12. leaves/leave) the house at 3:30, and (13. works/work) from 4:00 a.m. to noon. Then he (14. comes/come) home, (15. has/have) lunch, and (16. goes/go) to bed at 7:00 p.m.

Javier is a waiter at the restaurant. He (17. begins /begin) work at 5:00 p.m. He (18. doesn't go/don't go) to bed until late at night. He (19. stays/stay) in bed until almost noon. He (20. takes/take) the bus to work at 4:30 p.m. When he (21. comes/come) home, his uncle Ernesto is in bed.

Javier and Ernesto (22. doesn't work/don't work) on Sundays and Mondays. They (23. doesn't do/don't do) anything on those days. They just (24. stays/stay) home and (25. relaxes/relax).

B Javier is talking about his uncle Ernesto. Use the verbs in parentheses to complete the sentences. Pay attention to the spelling of the verbs.

1. (try)   My uncle _____ to help me.

2. (worry)   He _____ about me a lot.

3. (enjoy)   His job is difficult, but he _____ it a lot.

4. (watch)   On Sundays, he _____ TV.

5. (wash)   After dinner, he _____ the dishes.

6. (play)   On the weekend, he _____ soccer.

7. (study)   Sometimes he _____ English.

8. (do)   My uncle _____ a lot of things for me.

9. (miss)   I think he _____ Mexico.

10. (have)   He's happy, but he _____ a hard life.

C The information in this exercise is wrong. Look at Exercise A and correct the information.

1. Ernesto works during the evening.

   Ernesto doesn't work during the evening. He works in the morning.

2. Ernesto leaves the house at 3:00 a.m.

   _____

3. Javier wakes up at 3:00 a.m.

   _____

4. Juan and Ernesto come from Peru.

   _____

5. They work in different restaurants.

   _____

6. Javier does a lot of work on Sundays.

   _____

7. Ernesto has lunch at work.

   _____

D Write six sentences on a separate piece of paper. Write about three things you do every day. Write about three things you *don't* do every day. Then share your sentences with a partner.

EXAMPLE: *I wash the dishes every day.*
             I don't speak English every day.

Write six sentences about your partner.

EXAMPLE: *Julia washes the dishes every day.*
             Julia doesn't speak English every day.

Present Tense—*Wh* and Yes-No Questions

Do and does are "helping verbs." They help make questions. In questions, always use the base form of the main verb. Do not add *s*.

Does he **work**?   Where *do* they **work**?

Yes-No Questions			Short Answers	
Helping Verb	**Subject**	**Main Verb**		
Do	you	have a job?	Yes, I do.	No, I don't.
Does	he	have a job?	Yes, he does.	No, he doesn't.

Wh Questions				Answers
Wh Word	**Helping Verb**	**Subject**	**Main Verb**	
What	does	Max	do?	He's a waiter.
Where	does	Max	work?	At a restaurant.
What hours	does	he	work?	From 9:00 to 5:00.
Why	does	he	like his job?	Because it's fun.
When	does	he	work?	Tuesdays through Saturdays.
How often	do	they	take breaks?	Every three hours.
How many days	do	waiters	work?	Five days a week.
What days	do	they/you	work	Monday through Friday.

A Listen as you read about Javier's job. Then listen to the questions and fill in the blanks. After you listen, answer the questions.

I am a waiter at the Calypso restaurant. I work five days a week, eight hours a day. My hours are from 5:00 p.m. to 1:00 a.m. I'm off on Sundays. And I don't work on Mondays because the restaurant is closed.

I set the tables and serve dinner. It's a busy restaurant. I serve about fifty meals a day. I make about seven dollars an hour, and I get a lot of tips. I like my job because I meet a lot of people every day and I speak a lot of English.

I like the other waiters at this restaurant. We take a break every three hours. We don't wear uniforms, but we have to wear white shirts. We never wear jeans.

I like my job because it's fun and I eat a lot of delicious food. But sometimes I get tired because I stand up for so many hours.

	Questions	Answers
1.	.... does Javier do?	He's a waiter.
2.	.... does Javier work?	....
3.	.... he work every day?	....
4.	.... he get tips?	....
5.	.... the waiters wear uniforms?	....
6.	.... days a week does he work?	....
7.	.... does he like his job?	....

B Use the words in parentheses to write yes-no questions. Then read the information about Javier again and write short answers.

1. (Javier/have) <u>Does Javier have</u> a good job?   <u>Yes, he does.</u>

2. (Javier/work) .... on Mondays? ....

3. (the waiters/take) .... breaks? ....

4. (many customers/come) .... to the restaurant? ....

5. (Javier/serve) .... breakfast? ....

6. (the waiters/wear) .... jeans? ....

C Work with a partner. If your partner has a job, ask "Questions about work." If not, ask "Questions about fun." Write one question for number seven. Then write a paragraph about your partner on a separate piece of paper.

Questions about work:	Questions about fun:
1. Where do you work?	**1.** Do you like movies?
2. Do you like your job?	**2.** What movies do you like?
3. What hours do you work?	**3.** Where do you watch movies?
4. What days do you work?	**4.** How often do you watch movies?
5. Do you speak English at your job?	**5.** What do you do on weekends?
6. Do you wear a uniform?	**6.** Do you like to play sports?
7.	**7.** ....

D Chant

Questions

What's his name?
    His name is Lee.
What does he teach?
    He teaches history.
When does he teach?
    From one to three.
Does he teach on Fridays?
    Don't ask me.

What's her name?
    Her name is Sue.
Do you know her very well?
    Yes, I do.

Do you like her?
    Yes, I do.
    I like her a lot
I do too.

Where do you live?
    I live near the zoo.
Do you hear the lions?
    Yes, I do.
When do they wake up?
    They wake up at four.
Do they keep you awake?
    Not anymore.

Frequency Adverbs
Do you ever/Are you ever

Use frequency adverbs to talk about how often something happens.

Always	—— 100%	
Almost always		
Usually		
Often		
Sometimes	—— 50%	
Rarely, Hardly Ever		
Never	—— 0%	

Put frequency adverbs *after* the verb *BE*.

Subject	*BE*	Frequency Adverb	
My son	is	often	late.

Put frequency adverbs *before* all other verbs.

Subject	Frequency Adverb	Verb
My son	never	does his homework.
I	usually	cook dinner.
It	hardly ever	snows in my city.

Use *ever* to ask yes-no questions about how often something happens.

	Question	Short Answer
BE:	Are you **ever** late for class?	Yes, I **sometimes** am.
Other Verbs:	Do you **ever** cook dinner?	No, I **hardly ever** do.

Language Notes

***Sometimes* can be in three places.**

BE:	Sam is *sometimes* early. *Sometimes* Sam is early. Sam is early *sometimes*.
Other Verbs:	I *sometimes* cook dinner. *Sometimes* I cook dinner. I cook dinner *sometimes*.

***Often* can come at the end of a sentence.**

BE:	Sam is late *often*.
Other Verbs:	I cook dinner *often*.

A Julia is complaining about her son, Sam, to her neighbor, Mark. Read the conversation. Then listen and circle the words you hear.

Mark: How's your son Sam?
Julia: Oh, he's fine, but he's very lazy. He (1. never/hardly ever/usually) does his homework! He goes to bed so late that he's (2. always/often/usually) tired in the morning. Of course, he's (3. always/often/usually) late for school. And he (4. always/hardly ever/never) gets As on his report card!
Mark: Does he ever help you around the house?
Julia: He (5. never/rarely/sometimes) does! When he has free time, he (6. always/almost always/usually) plays on the computer. When he takes off his clothes, he (7. always/sometimes/usually) leaves them on the floor. He (8. never/hardly ever/sometimes) picks them up. I don't know what to do.
Mark: Do you ever punish him?
Julia: (9. Sometimes/Hardly ever/Never).
Mark: Hmm. Maybe that's the problem!

B Write the words in the correct order.

1. hardly ever/punishes/Julia/her son

Julia hardly ever punishes her son. ....

2. Sam/tired/usually/is

....

3. Sam/late/for school/is/ always

....

4. Sam/his clothes/leaves/usually/on the floor

....

5. Julia/often/angry/is/at her son

....

6. never/Sam/his mother/helps

....

C Write these sentences again using a frequency adverb. Write true sentences about your life.

1. I do my homework.   I usually do my homework. ....

2. I'm late for school.   ....

3. I go to bed late.   ....

4. I watch TV in English.   ....

5. We speak English in class.   ....

6. It snows in my city.   ....

D Write questions with *Are you ever* or *Do you ever*. Then ask a partner the questions and write short answers.

EXAMPLE:

Do you ever speak English outside of class?   Sometimes.

Are you ever homesick?   No, I never am.

Question		Short Answer
1. Do you ever	cook dinner?	....
2.	late for class?	....
3.	homesick?	....
4.	eat junk food?	....
5.	read in English?	....
6.	speak English outside of class?	....

Now write longer sentences about your partner on a separate piece of paper.

EXAMPLE: Rosa sometimes speaks English outside of class.

Contrast: Possessive 's, Contracted 's, and Plural s

An *s* at the end of a word can show different things.

Possessive 's   My sister'<u>s</u> friend has tickets.
Incorrect: ~~My sister friend has tickets.~~

Contracted 's   The show'<u>s</u> tonight. (=The show is tonight.)
Incorrect: ~~The show tonight.~~

Plural s   We have two ticket<u>s</u>.
Incorrect: ~~We have two ticket's.~~

Language Note: We can use possessive 's with time words.

yesterday's class   today's show   tomorrow's performance

A Charlie and Annie want to buy tickets to a concert. Read the conversation. What kind of *s* is in the underlined words? Write *poss* over each possessive *'s*. Write *is* over each contracted *'s*. Write *pl* over each plural *s*. Then listen to the conversation.

Charlie: Do you have two tickets to <u>tonight's</u> (*poss*) performance?

Clerk: I'm sorry. The <u>show's</u> (*is*) sold out tonight.

Charlie: How about tomorrow <u>afternoon's</u> show?

Clerk: Let me check. Well, <u>there's</u> a seat available on the side. Another <u>seat's</u> available in the front. I also have two <u>seats</u> together in the back.

Charlie: Let me see. Hey, Annie. <u>It's</u> sold out, but <u>tomorrow's</u> show has <u>tickets</u>.

Annie: We can't go tomorrow!

Charlie: Why not?

Annie: Remember? My <u>brother's</u> in a play tomorrow afternoon.

Charlie: Oh, but <u>Suzanne's</u> my favorite singer. I can't miss <u>Suzanne's</u> concert. <u>She's</u> here only once a year.

Annie: But my <u>brother's</u> the star of the play! I can't miss my <u>brother's</u> play!

Charlie: OK, OK, I'll go with you to the play.

B Charlie and Annie are at the play. Fill in the blanks with *s* or *'s*. Then circle each possessive *'s* and underline each contracted *'s*.

1. Charlie: Well. Your brother _'s_ a very good actor.

2. Annie: I think so, too. I think all the actor _____ are excellent.

3. Charlie: Are your parent _____ here?

4. Annie: Of course! My mother _____ in the front row,

5. and my father _____ over there with the movie camera.

6. My brother _____ girlfriend is next to my mother.

7. Charlie: I'm glad I came. It _____ a wonderful show.

8. Annie: Thanks for coming. I'll treat you to Suzanne _____ concert next year.

C Walk around the room. Ask your classmates these questions. When students say "Yes," ask them to write their first names on the lines. When they say "No," move on to another student. Choose a different student for each question.

	Students who answer "Yes"
1. Is your birthday this month?	....
2. Are you married?	....
3. Do your parents live in the U.S.?	....
4. Are you from a large city?	....
5. Is your city famous?	....

D Look at Exercise C. Write five sentences about your classmates. Use contracted *'s* when it is possible. Then circle each possessive *'s* and underline each contracted *'s*.

EXAMPLE: Linda's birthday's this month. Martin's married.

....

....

....

....

....

Review

Present Tense—Affirmative, Negative, Yes-No Questions, 'S vs. S

A **Dictation** Mike is talking about his life. Listen and write what you hear. Then circle the present tense verbs. Key words: *hardly, bored, during, until*

I have

B Rewrite the dictation. Change *I* to *He*.

Mike has a very exciting life. He

C Mike and his sister Linda are in the same class. They disagree about many things. Complete Linda's sentences. Write negative statements.

1. **Mike:** Our parents have a very easy life

   Linda: That's not true! They don't have an easy life!

2. **Mike:** Dad likes to wear jeans.

   Linda: That's not true! Dad

3. **Mike:** You need to study more.

   Linda: That's not true! I

4. **Mike:** Our teacher speaks our language.

   Linda: That's not true! Our teacher

5. **Mike:** Our teacher gives us too much homework.

   Linda: That's not true!

D Rewrite these sentences with frequency adverbs to create *true* sentences about yourself.

1. I go to bed late. <u>Sometimes I go to bed late.</u>

2. I'm late for class. ....

3. I take vitamins. ....

4. I go out for dinner. ....

5. I'm homesick. ....

6. I'm lazy. ....

7. I cook dinner. ....

8. I dream in English. ....

E Change the statements in Exercise D to yes-no questions with *ever*. Then ask a partner the questions. Circle your partner's answers.

1. <u>Do you ever go to bed late?</u>   Yes, I do.   No, I don't.

2. ....   Yes, I am.   No, I'm not.

3. ....   Yes, I do.   No, I don't.

4. ....   Yes, I do.   No, I don't.

5. ....   Yes, I am.   No, I'm not.

6. ....   Yes, I am.   No, I'm not.

7. ....   Yes, I do.   No, I don't.

8. ....   Yes, I do.   No, I don't.

F Find the mistakes. Rewrite the sentences.

1. My mother name is Sylvia.   <u>My mother's name is Sylvia.</u>

2. She live in Mexico. ....

3. She have a good job. ....

4. She doesn't has free time. ....

5. Always she works hard. ....

6. How often she visit you? ....

7. Never she visit me. ....

8. She no have time to visit me. ....

9. Tomorrow is my mother birthday. ....

10. She sixty years old. ....

Have Fun

A **Tic Tac Toe** Ask your classmates if they do the following things around the house. When a classmate answers "Yes," write his or her first name on the line. The first person to get three names in a straight line, vertical (|), horizontal (—), or diagonal (/) (\), is the winner.

EXAMPLE: *A: Do you ever wash the dishes?*
            B: Yes, I do.
            A: What's your name?
            B: Mark.

wash the dishes	shop for groceries	make your bed
....	....	....
cook dinner	take out the garbage	do the laundry
....	....	....
clean the bathroom	vacuum the floors	hang up your clothes
....	....	....

B **Guessing Game** Write about what a member of your family does. Write two *true* sentences and one *false* sentence. Use frequency adverbs in your sentences. Read your sentences to a small group or to your class. Your classmates will guess the sentence that is *false*.

EXAMPLE:

You	*My father often flies to Chicago. He sometimes loses his keys. He often cooks dinner.*
Your classmate:	*I don't think he flies to Chicago.*
You:	*You're wrong. He does. He flies to Chicago three times a year.*
Another classmate:	*He doesn't often cook dinner.*
You:	*That's right! He never cooks dinner.*

C Chant

He's Always Late

He's always late to his English class.
He never gets to class on time.
    Is Melissa ever late?
No, she isn't.
She always gets to class on time.
    What about you? Are you ever late?
Yes, I am, but it's not my fault.
Sometimes my alarm clock doesn't ring,
and I can't get to class on time.

Contrast: *BE* and *DO* in Present Tense Statements

Affirmative Statements with *BE*	Affirmative Statements with Other Verbs
Use *BE–am, is, are*–with nouns, adjectives and prepositional phrases. I'm a high school student. She's married. They're from Spain.	Don't use *BE* before verbs in the present tense. I have two children. She plays soccer. They love music.

Correct: I have two children.
Incorrect: I'm have two children.

Negative statements with *BE*	Negative statements with *DO*
Use *BE–am not, isn't, aren't*–with nouns, adjectives and prepositional phrases. He isn't good at sports. They aren't lazy.	Use *DO–doesn't, don't*–before verbs in the present tense. He doesn't play soccer. They don't study hard.

Correct: They aren't lazy.
Incorrect: They don't lazy.

Correct: He doesn't play soccer.
Incorrect: He isn't play soccer.

A Read the paragraphs below. Circle the correct choices. Then listen to check your answers.

My name is Sara. I (1. am/ø) have two children, Paula and Henry. They (2. are/ø) both in high school They (3. are/ø) speak perfect English.

Paula is the oldest. She (4. is/ø) very good at sports, but she (5. isn't/doesn't) a very good student. She (6. isn't/doesn't) like to do her homework. She (7. is/ø) plays soccer for her school. Her room (8. is/ø) full of trophies. Paula (9. is/ø) wants to be in the Olympics some day. She (10. isn't/doesn't) want to go to college.

Henry (11. isn't/doesn't) athletic. He (12. isn't/doesn't) like to play any sports. But he (13. is/ø) loves music. He (14. is/ø) practices the piano five hours a day, so he (15. isn't/doesn't) have much time for schoolwork. He (16. is/ø) plays classical music and jazz. He (17. is/ø) very talented.

B The information in these sentences is not correct. Make the affirmative sentences negative and the negative sentences affirmative.

1. Sara and her family live in New York. *They don't live in New York.*

2. Paula and Henry don't speak English. ....

3. Paula and Henry are teachers. ....

4. Henry is good at sports. ....

5. Henry doesn't play the piano. ....

6. Paula wants to be a singer. ....

7. The children aren't talented. ....

C Henry is talking about himself and his family. Fill in the blanks to make negative statements.

1. I *'m not* .... married.

2. I .... have a guitar.

3. I .... good at sports.

4. My family .... live in a big house.

5. I .... like loud music.

6. Baseball .... my favorite sport.

7. My sister and I .... famous.

8. I .... need to learn English.

D It's ten years later. Paula is now married. Read the following paragraph. Underline the verb in each sentence. Then write the paragraph again. Make the sentences negative.

I'm married. I <u>live</u> in a big house. It has ten rooms. The rooms have expensive furniture.

My husband is the president of a computer company. He makes a lot of money. He buys me diamonds every day. I have a lot of jewels!

We're very rich. We travel all over the world. Our life is very comfortable... but we're bored!

I'm not married. I don't live in a big house.

....

....

....

....

....

....

Contrast: *BE* and *DO* in Present Tense Yes-No Questions

BE is a verb. Use *BE* with nouns, adjectives, and prepositional phrases. To make a Yes-No question with *BE*, put a form of *BE* before the subject.

BE	Subject	Adjective/Noun/ Prepositional Phrase	Short Answers	
Am	I	on time?	Yes, you are.	No, you aren't./No, you're not.
Is	he	a good dancer?	Yes, he is.	No, he isn't./No, he's not.
Are	you	happy?	Yes, I am.	-------------/No, I'm not.

To make a Yes-No question with all other verbs, put *DO* or *DOES* before the subject. *DO* is a helping verb.

Helping Verb	Subject	Main Verb		Short Answers	
Do	you	like	parties?	Yes, I do.	No, I don't.
Does	it	rain	a lot?	Yes, it does.	No, it doesn't.

Language Notes

Do not use *BE* before other verbs in present tense questions.

Correct	Incorrect
Do you like parties?	~~Are you like parties?~~
Does your teacher help you?	~~Is your teacher help you?~~

Do not use *DO* before adjectives.

Correct	Incorrect
Are you happy?	~~Do you happy?~~

A Look at the Personality Test below. Complete the questions with *Are you* or *Do you*. Then listen to check your answers. Finally, answer the questions with *true* short answers about yourself.

WHAT KIND OF PERSON ARE YOU? TAKE THIS TEST AND FIND OUT!

1. _Are you_ usually happy? ....

2. .... go to many parties? ....

3. .... enjoy quiet places? ....

4. .... read a lot every day? ....

5. .... often on the phone? ....

6. .... often late for school? ....

7. .... eat at restaurants alone? ....

8. .... like to be alone? ....

Now look at your answers to the Personality Test. Read the following explanation of the test and circle a choice below.

If you answered YES to #1, 2 ,5, and 6, you are probably a very social person.
If you answered YES to #3, 4, 7, and 8, you are probably an independent person who enjoys being alone.

What kind of person are you?
a. I am a social person.
b. I am an independent person.

B Look at the underlined words in the questions below. What is underlined in each sentence—a prepositional phrase, an adjective, a noun, or the main verb? Check (✓) the correct column. Circle the forms of BE and DO.

	Prepositional Phrase	Adjective	Noun	Main Verb
1. (Are) you usually <u>happy</u>?	....	✔	....	....
2. Do you <u>have</u> a big family?	....	....	....	....
3. Are you a good <u>dancer</u>?	....	....	....	....
4. Are you <u>afraid</u> to speak English?	....	....	....	....
5. Do you <u>miss</u> your family?	....	....	....	....
6. Are you often <u>homesick</u>?	....	....	....	....
7. Are you always <u>on time</u>?	....	....	....	....

C Complete the following questions. Then ask a partner the questions. Your partner will think of a country and answer your questions. Try to guess the country your partner is thinking about.

Questions	Answers
1. ..... Is ..... the country in Asia?	....
2. .... it in South America?	....
3. .... it a big country?	....
4. .... many people live there?	....
5. .... people speak Spanish in this country?	....
6. .... this country famous for soccer?	....

I know! The country is ....!

Contrast: *BE* and *DO* in Present Tense *Wh* Questions

To make a *Wh* Question with *BE*, use a Question Word + *BE* + subject.

Question Word	*BE*	Subject
Where	is	San Francisco?
What	is	San Francisco famous for?
How much	are	the tickets?

To make *Wh* Questions with all other verbs, use a Question Word + *DO* or *DOES* + subject + main verb.

Question Word	Helping Verb	Subject	Main Verb
What	do	people	love to do in San Francisco?
What	does	the name	mean?
Why	do	many tourists	come to San Francisco?
How much	do	the tickets	cost?

Language Note
Do not use *BE* with other verbs in the present tense.

Correct	Incorrect
What *does* the name mean?	~~What is the name mean?~~
How much *do* the tickets cost?	~~How much are the tickets cost?~~

A Listen to Susan's report about San Francisco. Write *is*, *do* or *does* to complete the questions below. Then listen to check your answers.

San Francisco is a beautiful city in California. The name San Francisco means "Saint Francis" in Spanish.

San Francisco is famous for its Golden Gate Bridge. But it is also famous for high prices. Hotels often cost more than $200 a night.

People in San Francisco love to eat at good restaurants. They also love to visit the beautiful parks and beaches.

The weather in San Francisco is strange for many people. It's very foggy. And it's very cold in the summer. But many tourists come to San Francisco because it is a very beautiful city.

1. Where _____ San Francisco?

2. What _____ the name *San Francisco* mean?

3. What _____ San Francisco famous for?

4. How much _____ hotels cost in San Francisco?

5. What _____ people love to do in San Francisco?

6. How _____ the weather in San Francisco?

7. Why _____ many tourists come to San Francisco?

B Look at the movie theatre sign in San Francisco. Complete the questions with *where / what time / how much* and a form of *BE* or *DO*.

MATINEE: 2:30 p.m.
EVENING SHOW: 8:00 p.m.
FREE PARKING NEXT DOOR
150 GEARY STREET

EVENING
$12.00 ADULTS
$8.00 CHILDREN UNDER 16

MATINEE
$8.00 ADULTS
$6.00 CHILDREN UNDER 16

1. .... the movie begin?

It begins at 8:00 P.M.

2. .... the movie theater?

It's on Geary Street.

3. .... tickets for the matinee?

Tickets are $8.00 for adults and $6.00 for children under sixteen.

4. .... tickets cost for the evening show?

Tickets cost $12.00 for adults and $8.00 for children under sixteen.

5. .... the parking lot?

The parking lot is next to the theater.

6. .... parking cost?

It's free!

C Complete the following questions with *is, are, does,* or *do.* Then ask a partner the questions and write down his or her answers.

Questions	Your partner's answers
1. What .... your favorite city?	....
2. What .... its name mean?	....
3. What .... it famous for?	....
4. What .... people like to do there?	....
5. How .... the weather there?	....
6. What .... your favorite places there?	....

 D Chant

How Much Does a Taxi Cost in Peru?

How much does a taxi cost in Peru?
How much is a dinner in Lima for two?
How's the weather in December in Timbuktu?
How long does it take to fly to Katmandu?

How long does it take to walk across France?
Where's the best school in Paris to learn to dance?
Where do you shop for clothes in Nice?
What do you wear in the summer in Greece?

Contrast: Subject Pronouns, Object Pronouns, and Possessive Adjectives

Subject Pronouns	Object Pronouns	Possessive Adjectives
I you he she it we they	me you him her it us them	my your his her its our their
Before verbs:	**After most verbs and after prepositions:**	**Before nouns:**
I see the students.	The students see me. He is in front of me.	Morgan is my neighbor.

A Heather is introducing us to her neighbors. Circle the correct words in each sentence. Then listen to check your answers.

1. (Me/**My**) name is Heather. My parents and (I/me) live in this house. We like the neighborhood, but (we/it) have problems with some of (our/your) neighbors.

2. This is Mr. Parker. (He/Him) lives next door to (we/us). (He/Him) plays the trumpet every morning at 6:00 a.m. We like (he/him), but we don't like (he's/his) trumpet.

3. This is Morgan and (his/her) wife Susie. (They/She) live next door to Mr. Parker. We have problems with (they/them) because (he/they) have a very unfriendly dog. (They/Their) dog barks every night.

4. This is Mrs. Rivera. She lives across the street from (we/us). (She/He) is eighty years old. We like (she/her) because she bakes chocolate chip cookies for (we/us) every Sunday. (Her/ Hers) cookies are delicious!

B Use the information from Exercise A to answer these questions. Use subject and object pronouns for the underlined words.

1. When does <u>Mr. Parker</u> play <u>his trumpet</u>?

He plays it _____ every morning.

2. When does <u>Mrs. Rivera</u> bake <u>chocolate chip cookies</u>?

_____ bakes _____ every Sunday.

3. Does <u>Heather</u> like <u>the neighborhood</u>?

Yes, _____ likes _____ very much.

4. How do <u>Heather and her parents</u> feel about <u>the neighbors</u>?

_____ have problems with some of _____.

5. Does <u>Mrs. Rivera</u> live next door to <u>Heather and her parents</u>?

No, _____ doesn't live next door to _____.

6. Do <u>Morgan and Susie</u> live across the street from <u>Mrs. Rivera</u>?

No, _____ don't live across the street from _____.

C Read the conversations between the neighbors. Complete the sentences. Use the words in parentheses. You can use some words more than once.

1. (you, your, it)

Heather: Mrs. Rivera, where did ____you____ buy _____ hat?

Mrs. Rivera: I bought _____ in Hawaii.

Heather: _____ looks good on _____.

2. (he, him, his)

Mrs. Rivera: I think Mr. Parker is very strange. _____ plays _____ trumpet so early in the morning!

Heather: We should talk to _____ about that.

3. (we, our, us)

Heather: Hi. Are you _____ new neighbors?

Jane and John: Yes, _____ live down the street. _____ address is 22 Oak Street.

Heather: Welcome to the neighborhood. Please visit _____ some time!

Jane and John: Thanks!

4. (it, they, them, their)

Heather: How do you like the neighborhood?

Jane and John: We like _____ very much. _____'s very safe.

Heather: Have you met all the neighbors?

John: Well, we met Morgan and Susie. _____ seem very nice, but _____ dog isn't very friendly.

Heather: I know!

Review

DO vs. BE in the Present Tense

A **Dictation** Listen to Mary talk about her son John. Write what you hear. After you write, circle the verbs. Key words: *lucky, healthy, As*

My son is very lucky.

B Rewrite the dictation. Change all the sentences to negative statements.

My son is not very lucky.

C Do you have a lucky number? Do you have a lucky color? Read the following paragraph. Complete the questions with *is, are, does,* or *do.* Then write the answers. Write long answers for numbers 4, 6, and 7.

Many cultures have lucky and unlucky numbers. In the U.S., the number 13 is an unlucky number. For example, people think that bad things happen on Friday, the 13th. Also, many buildings in the United States don't have a 13th floor. In some Asian countries, the number 4 is unlucky because the word 'four' in many Asian languages means 'death.'

Some colors are lucky in certain countries. For example, in China, people think the color red is very lucky. Many brides wear red when they get married. In the U.S., brides usually wear white.

1. Question: _Is_ the number 13 a lucky number in the U.S.?
   Answer: _No, it isn't._

2. Question: _____ all buildings have 13th floors in the United States?
   Answer: _____

3. Question: _____ 4 a lucky number in Asia?
   Answer: _____

4. Question: What _____ the word '4' mean in some Asian countries?
   Answer: _____

5. Question: _____ red a lucky color in China?
   Answer: _____

6. Question: What color _____ brides wear in China?

Answer: _____

7. Question: What numbers _____ lucky in your country?

Answer: _____

D Read these sentences. If the information is correct, write *"That's true!"* If the information is wrong, write *"That's not true."* If the sentence is not true, rewrite it and make it negative.

1. Brides wear orange in the United States.

That's not true. Brides don't wear orange in the United States.

2. Many American brides get married in June.

That's true!

3. The number 13 is lucky in the U.S.

_____

4. American students stand up when the teacher comes in the room.

_____

5. The colors of the American flag are red, white and blue.

_____

6. The President of the United States lives in New York.

_____

E Complete the chart.

Affirmative	Negative	Yes-No Question
I want to learn English.	I don't want to learn English.	Do you want to learn English?
He wants to learn English.		
I'm worried about my English.		
He's worried about his English.		

F Read the paragraph. Then rewrite it on a separate piece of paper. Change the underlined nouns to subject pronouns (*he, she, it, we, they*), or object pronouns (*him, her, it, us, them*).

My brother has a new car. The new car is beautiful, but the new car cost a lot of money. My brother's wife doesn't like the new car because my brother's wife thinks that the new car was too expensive. My brother's wife wants my brother to return the new car. I agree with my brother's wife. My brother's wife and I think that my brother should return the car! But my brother won't listen to my brother's wife and me. What should my brother and my brother's wife do?

FIRST SENTENCE: *My brother has a new car. It is beautiful, but...*

Have Fun

A *Find Someone Who* **Bingo** Complete the yes-no questions for all of the items on the bingo card. Then walk around the classroom and ask your questions. When a student says *yes*, write his or her first name under the question. The first person to have five names in a straight line, vertical (|), horizontal (—), or diagonal (/) (\), is the winner.

Do you	....	....	....	....
work in a restaurant?	have a computer?	older than I am?	go to the library?	live with your family?
good at math?	live alone?	have a roommate?	live far from school?	speak three languages?
speak four languages?	like to cook?	FREE SPACE	a U.S. citizen?	married?
love to plant flowers?	under 21 years old?	have a pet?	exercise every day?	buy a lot of clothes?
play a musical instrument?	happy?	often come to class late?	like chocolate?	like to read?

B **Word Game** Join a team of three or four students. Look at the letters in the box below. Your team will have five minutes to make as many nouns, verbs, and prepositions as you can from the letters in the box. You can use letters more than one time in each word. At the end of the five minutes, the team with the most words wins.

B	A	D	I
E	R	U	L
T	S	C	O
M	N	P	F

Nouns	Verbs	Prepositions
ear	do	in

C Chant

Sally's Sister

Sally's sister doesn't like to cook.
She likes to sit down
And read a good book.
She's a wonderful student
And she's very sweet.
She doesn't like to cook
But she loves to eat.

   Do you know her brother?
Yes, I do. He talks about the weather on Channel Two.
   Is he very handsome?
No, he's not, but he's very smart and he reads a lot.

LESSON 20

Present Continuous Tense—Affirmative and Negative Statements

Use the present continuous tense to talk about what is happening right now or to talk about a future plan. The present continuous tense has two parts: *BE* and verb + *ing*. In the present continuous tense, *BE* is a helping verb.

	PART 1	PART 2
I	am	
You/They/We	are	sitting in the classroom. (present)
He/She/It	is	leaving at 2:00. (future)

A negative statement in the present continuous has three parts: *BE*, not, and verb + *ing*.

	PART 1	PART 2	PART 3
I	am		
You/They/We	are	not	sitting in the park. (present)
He/She/It	is		leaving at 1:00. (future)

Spelling of verb + –*ing*:

1. Add *ing* to most verbs.   wait–waiting

2. When a verb ends in C + *e* , drop   live–living
    (don't use) the *e*. Add *ing*

3. When a verb has one syllable and ends   sit–sitting
    in CVC, double the last consonant and add *ing*.

4. Do not double the last consonant when a verb:

    a. ends in *w, x,* or *y*   fix–fixing

    b. ends in VVC   eat–eating

    c. has two or more syllables with   vísit–vís-it-ing
        stress on the first syllable.

Reminder

C = Consonant
V = Vowel
CVC = Consonant + Vowel + Consonant
VVC = Vowel + Vowel + Consonant

A Listen to the telephone conversations. Write the number of the conversation under each picture.

A.

B.

C.

D.

....

B Complete the telephone conversations below with the present continuous tense forms of the verbs in the box. Use each word once.

come	have	make	read	talk	watch
do	go	rain	take	wait	win

1. A: Hello. Can I speak to Mary?

    B: I'm sorry. Can you call back? She _____is taking_____ a shower.

2. A: Hi. How's the weather in Chicago?

    B: It _____ and my umbrella is broken!

3. A: So, how is your vacation?

    B: Great! We _____ wonderful time.

4. A: Hello. Is Ray there?

    B: One minute. Ray! Telephone!

    C: Shhh! Not now. I _____ the game on TV. The score is 4 to 3, and the Yankees _____!

5. A: Susan! Get off the phone! I _____ for a phone call.

    B: I (negative) _____ on the phone, Dad. I _____ a book.

    A: Oh, sorry.

6. A: When is your brother's trip to Mexico?

    B: He _____ next month.

7. A: Where are you? You're so late!

    B: I _____. I'll be there in a minute!

8. A: How are your children?

    B: They're great. They _____ their homework right now.

9. A: Hi, What are you doing? Do you want to take a walk?

    B: I can't now. I _____ some chocolate chip cookies.

C Ask three classmates these questions. Put their answers in the chart.

Name	What are you doing after class?	What are you doing this weekend?
Martin	I'm going to the library.	I'm taking a trip.

Now write sentences about your classmates on a separate piece of paper.

EXAMPLE: Martin is going to the library after class today.

Present Continuous Tense—Questions

Use Yes-No questions in the present continuous tense to ask if something is happening right now or to ask about a future plan.

Questions	Short Answers		
	Affirmative (No contraction)	Negative	
Am I working?	Yes, you are.	No, you aren't.	No, you're not.
Are you coming home tomorrow?	Yes, I am. Yes, we are.	--- No, we aren't.	No, I'm not. No, we're not.
Is he/she studying?	Yes, he/she is.	No, he/she isn't.	No, he's/she's not.
Is it raining?	Yes, it is.	No, it isn't.	No, it's not.
Are we having dinner at 8:00?	Yes, we are. Yes, you are.	No, we aren't. No, you aren't.	No, we're not. No, you're not.
Are they coming home?	Yes, they are.	No, they aren't.	No, they're not.

Ask *Wh* Questions in the present continuous tense to get information about what is happening right now, or to ask about a future plan.

Questions	Answers
What are you doing?	I'm/We're studying.
Where is he going?	To the movies.
Why are they studying English?	Because they want to.
How am I doing?	Fine!
Who is she talking to?	Her mother.
When are you leaving?	On Tuesday.

A Bob and Susan are in Florida with their new baby. Susan's mother is in Boston. Complete the questions. Then listen to Susan's conversation with her mother and match the questions with the answers.

1. What .... Bob doing?   **a.** Talking on the phone.

2. What .... Susan doing?   **b.** Her mother.

3. .... they having a good time? **c.** Yes, it is.

4. What .... the baby doing?   **d.** Cooking hamburgers.

5. When .... they coming home?   **e.** Crying.

6. .... it raining in Boston?   **f.** Next Monday.

7. Who .... Susan talking to?   **g.** Yes, they are.

B Look at the picture in Exercise A. Write yes-no questions in the present continuous tense with the words below. Write short answers.

	Questions	Answers
1. the baby/sleep	Is the baby sleeping?	Yes, she is.
2. Susan/work hard		
3. the sun/shine		
4. Susan and Bob/ have a good time		
5. Bob/talk on the phone		

C Look at the picture in Exercise A. Write *Wh* questions for the answers.

1. Susan's mother: _What is Bob cooking?_

Susan: Bob's cooking hamburgers.

2. Susan's mother: _____

Susan: I'm wearing shorts.

3. Susan's mother: _____

Susan: I'm sitting outside.

4. Bob: _____

Susan: I'm talking to my mother.

D Write a sentence about something important that you're doing these days.

EXAMPLES: I'm looking for a new job.
              I'm taking an art class.

These days = now, at this time

Your sentence: _____

Now ask three classmates, "What are you doing these days?"
Write their answers in the chart.

Name of Classmate	What is he/she doing these days?
Miki	Miki is learning how to play the piano.
1.	
2.	
3.	

Contrast: Present and Present Continuous Tenses

See Appendix E for more time expressions.

Use the present tense to talk about something that repeats or is routine.	Use the present continuous tense to talk about what is happening right now or about a future plan.
They usually **play** soccer. Do they usually **play** soccer? What do they usually **play**?	They're **playing** soccer now. Are they **playing** soccer now? Why are they **playing** soccer?

Some Time Expressions

Present Tense	Present Continuous Tense
• every… second, minute, hour, day, week, weekend, month, year, Monday • once a day, twice a week, three times a month • on Tuesdays • always, usually, sometimes, rarely, never	• now • right now • today, tomorrow, at noon, at 6:00 • this …week, weekend, month, year • these days

A A reporter is asking people about their hobbies. Read the following interviews. Circle the verbs in the present tense. Underline the verbs in the present continuous tense. Then listen.

Interviewer:	Today our question is "What do you do in your spare time?" I'm at the mall and I'm going to talk to a few shoppers. Excuse me. What's your name?
Tina:	My name is Tina.
Interviewer:	What do you do in your spare time?
Tina:	I knit. I'm in a knitting club. It meets every Saturday. Right now I'm knitting a sweater for my son. I'm working hard on it.

Interviewer:	Thank you, Tina. And you two young men… what are your names?
Jake:	My name is Jake and this is my brother, Tom.
Interviewer:	And what do you do in your spare time?
Jake:	We love sports. We play soccer in the fall and tennis in the spring. But we don't play any sports in the winter.

Interviewer:	And what's your name, sir?
Charlie:	My name is Charlie.
Interviewer:	What do you do in your spare time?
Charlie:	I read a lot. I buy a new book every week. I usually read mysteries. I don't like love stories. Right now I'm reading Sherlock Holmes stories.

B Complete the sentences with the verbs in parentheses. Use the present or present continuous tense. Check (✔) PT for present tense and PCT for present continuous tense.

		PT	PCT
1.	Tina (knit) .... every Saturday.	....	....
2.	Right now she (knit) .... a sweater.	....	....
3.	Her knitting club (meet) .... once a week.	....	....
4.	Jake and his brother (play) .... soccer in the fall.	....	....
5.	They (not play) .... soccer in the spring.	....	....

C Complete the following chart with sentences and questions in the present tense and the present continuous tense.

	Present Tense	**Present Continuous Tense**
Affirmative Singular	Richard listens to jazz every day.	Richard is listening to jazz now.
Affirmative Plural	His parents ......_take_...... a walk every day.	His parents .... a walk now.
Negative Singular	Richard .... to jazz every day.	Richard isn't listening to jazz now.
Negative Plural	His parents .... a walk every day.	His parents .... a walk now.
Yes-No Question Singular	Does Richard listen to jazz every day?	.... he .... to jazz now?
Yes-No Question Plural	.... his parents .... a walk every day?	.... his parents .... a walk now?

D On a separate piece of paper, answer the questions, "What do you do in your spare time?" and "What are you doing these days?" Then ask three classmates these questions and write their answers.

EXAMPLE:
I read in my spare time. I'm working a lot these days.
Mona watches movies in her spare time. She is planning her wedding these days.

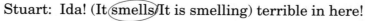

LESSON 23 Non-Action Verbs

Some verbs are not usually used in the present continuous tense. Use these verbs in the present tense to talk about what is happening right now.

Senses	Feelings	Opinion	Possession	Mental States	Other
feel	hate	agree	belong	forget	be
hear	like	believe	have	know	cost
look	love	disagree	own	remember	need
see		feel		understand	want
smell		think			
sound					
taste					

Reminder

Use do/does in present tense questions. Use am/is/are in present continuous tense questions.

Correct	**Incorrect**
I have a headache now.	~~I'm having a headache now.~~
She wants to paint the house.	~~She's wanting to paint the house.~~
Do you need more paint?	~~Are you needing more paint?~~

Some verbs can be both non-action verbs and action verbs.

Non-Action	**Action**
Do you have a car?	Are you having a good time?
I see a parking space!	I'm seeing my friend tomorrow.
You look great.	He's looking at a picture.
The flowers smell good.	I'm smelling the flowers.
The cake tastes delicious.	She's tasting the cake.

A Ida is painting the bathroom. Circle the correct choice in each of the following sentences. Listen to the conversation to check your answers.

Stuart: Ida! (It smells/It is smelling) terrible in here!
What (do you do/are you doing)?

Ida: (I paint/I'm painting) the walls.

Stuart: Why (do you paint/are you painting) the walls?

Ida: Because (they look/they're looking) terrible!

Stuart: But why (are you using/do you use) pink?
(I don't like/I'm not liking) pink.

Ida: But (I love/I'm loving) pink. Can you help me?
(I need/I'm needing) more paint.

Stuart: OK. But (I want/I'm wanting) to change the color.
How about gray?

Ida: Gray! (I hate/I'm hating) gray. Listen.
(The phone rings./The phone is ringing.) Will you get it?

Stuart: OK.

B Ida is talking to her friend Margaret on the phone. Use the verbs below in the present or present continuous tense.

cost	do	help	paint
cry	have	like	want

Margaret: Hi Ida! What _____are_____ you _____doing_____?

Ida: I _____ my bathroom right now.

Margaret: _____ your husband _____ you?

Ida: No, he isn't. He (negative) _____ the color pink.

Margaret: Maybe he'll change his mind. Listen. _____

you _____ to go shopping today? There's a sale at

Lynn's clothing store.

Ida: No, I'm sorry. I'm too busy. And Lynn's is very expensive. The

clothes _____ a lot of money. Oh, I have to go.

The baby _____ .

Margaret: Is she OK?

Ida: She's OK, but she _____ a cold. I'll talk to you later.

Margaret: OK. Bye!

C Find the mistakes. Rewrite the sentences.

1. Do you painting the room now? _Are you painting the room now?_

2. I'm need some help. _____

3. It's cost a lot of money. _____

4. They having a good time now. _____

5. Are you have a headache now? _____

6. Listen. The baby crying! _____

7. We don't having dinner now. _____

D Chant

I don't understand her.

Listen.
  I'm listening,
  But I don't understand her very well.
She's speaking in English.
  I know she is,
  But I don't understand her very well.

She's speaking very slowly.
  I know she is,
  But I don't understand her very well.
She's an interesting woman.
  I'm sure she is,
  But I don't understand her very well.

Review

Present Tense and Present Continuous Tense

A **Dictation** Maggie and Mark are talking to each other on the plane. Listen and write what you hear. Then circle the verbs in the simple present tense and underline the verbs in the present continuous tense. Key words: *spare, travel, cousin*

Mark: So, what (do) you (do) _____

Maggie: _____

_____

Mark: _____

Maggie: _____

_____

B Maggie is talking to a friend on the street in Toronto. Fill in each blank with the subject and the correct form of the verbs in parentheses.

> **Reminder**
>
> You can use the present continuous tense to talk about the future.

Donna: Hi Maggie! What a surprise! What (you/do) __are you doing__ here!

Maggie: (I/be) _____I'm_____ here for a business meeting. Also, (I/visit)

_____my cousin tomorrow. How (you/do) _____?

Are you still working at Morgan's?

Donna: No, (I/be not) _____. (I/be) _____ in school now.

(I/want) _____ to be an artist. How (be/your brother)

_____?

Maggie: (He/be) _____ OK, but (he/not have) _____ a job

right now.

Donna: That's too bad. (you/have) _____ time for coffee? (I/want)

_____ to talk to you some more.

Maggie: (I/not have) _____ time now, but how about dinner tonight?

Donna: I can't tonight. (I/have) _____ dinner with my boss. I'll call

you. What hotel (you/stay) _____ at?

Maggie: The Royal Hotel.

Donna: I know that hotel. I'll call you later.

C Read Donna's email to Maggie. Fill in each blank with the subject and the correct form of the verbs in parentheses.

From: Donna   To: Maggie
Subject: Hi from Toronto   Sent: 11/15/06 8:07 p.m.
Dear Maggie,

    I hope you had a good time here in Toronto. Dinner was fun.
(I/sit) <u>I'm sitting</u> in my room now. (I/try) .... to draw a
picture for my art class. (I/like) .... my art class, but (it/cost)
.... a lot of money. (I/want) .... to be an artist, but (my
father/not want) .... me to study art. (He/want)
.... me to be an accountant. (I/not know) .... what to do!
Oh well. (The phone/ring) .... I have to go! Call me.
Donna

D Which time words are usually used with the simple present? Which are usually used with the present continuous? Put each word or phrase in the correct column.

every day	now	on Mondays	usually
once a year	today	this month	this week

Simple Present

....
....
....
....

Present Continuous

....
....
....
....

E Write eight true sentences about yourself on a separate piece of paper. Use the verbs in the box in the present tense or present continuous tense. Use time words from Exercise D.

wear	need	go	do
want	study	take	sit

EXAMPLE: *I take the bus to school every day.*

Have Fun

A Find the Differences Work with a partner. Look at the pictures below. Write sentences about the differences between House A and House B.

House A   **House B**

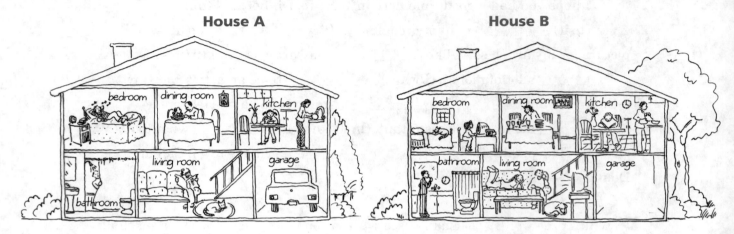

1. In house A, a man is taking a shower. In house B, a man is brushing his teeth.

2. _____

3. _____

4. _____

5. _____

6. _____

B Chant

Love Stories

Bill's in love with a girl named Sue,
But Sue's in love with his brother, Lou.
Lou loves Sally, but she doesn't know it.
He's crazy about her, but he doesn't show it.

Jim is waiting for a smile from Kim.
He loves her, but she doesn't love him.
Kim is thinking of a boy named Bill.
She loves him, but he loves Jill.

Jill loves her brother's good friend Ray,
but Ray's new love is a girl named Fay.
Fay's my friend. What more can I say?
I know she's in love, but not with Ray.

LESSON 24

Singular and Plural Nouns

See inside back cover for more spelling rules.

See Appendix G for special nouns.

Most nouns can be singular or plural.

Spelling of Regular Plural Nouns	Singular	Plural
1. Add *s* to most nouns.	a car an apartment	cars apartments
2. For nouns that end in *s*, *ss*, *ch*, *sh*, *x*, and *z*, add -*es*.	a dress an inch	dresses inches
3. For nouns that end in consonant + *y*, change the *y* to *i* and add -*es*.	a puppy a dictionary	puppies dictionaries
4. For nouns that end in f, change the *f* to *v* and add -*es*.	a shelf a wife	shelves wives

Irregular Plurals	Singular	Plural (do not add –s)
Some nouns have irregular plural forms. They do not end in *s*.	a man a woman a person a child	men women people children

Some nouns are always plural: *glasses, jeans, pants, shorts.*

A or An with singular nouns:

A and *an* = one. Use *a* and *an* with singular nouns.
Use *a* when the next word begins with a consonant sound (a h̲at, a n̲ew engine).
Use *an* when the next word starts with a vowel sound (an u̲mbrella, an o̲ld book).
Use *an* when the next word starts with a silent *h* (an h̲our, an h̲onest man).
Use *a* when *u* is pronounced *y* (a u̲niversity, a u̲sed book).
Use *one* only when you are counting (one book, two books).
Do not use *a* or *an* with plural nouns (correct: a book   Incorrect: a book̶s̶)

A Mimi and Rob are looking at newspaper ads. Underline the singular nouns. Circle the plural nouns. Then listen. Circle the ads Mimi and Rob are talking about.

a. I'm selling an old <u>truck</u>. It's only 10 years old. <u>It</u> has a new engine and new (brakes.) It's only $2,000. Call Ed 273-2252	**b.** Our beautiful dog is a new mom! We have three free puppies. They're very cute! Call Miranda 253-0994
c. I'm moving! I need boxes! I'm also selling a used car. Call Jerry 525-3003	**d.** I'm having a garage sale on July 5, 9:00 to 4:00, 456 Oak St. I have 2 bicycles, clocks, a rug, an answering machine, and toys. Call early!

B Here's a list of things that Mimi and Rob want. Write *a* or *an* on the lines next to singular nouns. Write "X" on the lines next to plural nouns.

1. _an_ old camera
2. _____ computer
3. _____ oriental rug
4. _____ bicycles
5. _____ antique clock
6. _____ answering machine
7. _____ English dictionary
8. _____ used books
9. _____ umbrellas

C Mimi and Rob are at the garage sale on Oak Street. Read the sentences and make the nouns plural.

1. There are a lot of (person) _____people_____ at the garage sale.

2. Some (woman) _____ are buying (toy) _____ for their (baby) _____.

3. Two strong (man) _____ are carrying heavy (box) _____.

4. Mimi is buying three (dish) _____ and two big (bookshelf) _____.

5. Three (child) _____ are playing with some (puppy) _____.

6. Some (boy) _____ are buying computer (game) _____.

D Find the mistakes. Rewrite the sentences.

1. The truck has new engine.   _The truck has a new engine._
2. Mimi and Bob want many thing.   _____
3. Mimi wants to get puppy.   _____
4. She needs new bicycle.   _____
5. They need more box.   _____
6. They are selling three puppys.   _____
7. Many peoples are here.   _____
8. The childrens have a lot of toys. _____
9. Mimi and Bob have apartment.   _____
10. They are new student in this school. _____

Count and Non-Count Nouns

See Appendix H for a list of non-count nouns.

There are two different kinds of nouns: count and non-count.

Count nouns have two forms: singular (used with *a* or *an*) or plural.

Singular: I need a ticket.   **Plural:** I need two tickets.

Non-count nouns have only one form. You can't count them. Don't use *a* or *an* with non-count nouns. Don't add *s* to non-count nouns.

Correct I need information.   **Incorrect:** ~~I need an informations.~~   ~~I need informations.~~

You can use either *the* or a possessive adjective (*my/your/his/her/its/our/their*) before both count nouns and non-count nouns.

Where's **the** ticket?   Where's **the** money?
Where's **my** ticket?   Where's **my** money?

Common Non-Count Nouns			**Food Non-Count Nouns**		
furniture	luggage	software	bread	fruit	rice
homework	money	traffic	cheese	gum	sugar
information	music	time	coffee	food	tea
jewelry	paper		candy	milk	water

Some and A lot of:

You can use *some* and *a lot of* with plural count nouns and non-count nouns.
Do not use *some* and *a lot of* with singular count nouns.

Correct: I have **some** magazines.   I have **some** money.
                 I have **a lot of** magazines.   I have **a lot of** money.
Incorrect: ~~I have some magazine.~~
                 ~~I have a lot of magazine.~~

A Tina's father, Stan, is going to give Tina a ride to the airport. Listen to the conversation. Then underline the count nouns and circle the non-count nouns.

Stan: Hurry Tina! There's a lot of (traffic) today! You don't want to be late.
Tina: I'm almost ready. I need to bring something to eat.
Stan: Well, take some fruit. There's a banana and an orange in the kitchen.
Tina: Thanks. I'll buy some coffee at the airport. And maybe some gum and a magazine. Now, let me see. I need to take some jewelry.
Stan: Don't bring any jewelry. You might lose it.
Tina: I'm bringing only one necklace and one bracelet…. Here they are!
Stan: OK. Do you have everything? Do you need some money?
Tina: I have a lot of money. And I have a credit card.
Stan: OK. Let's go. You have a lot of luggage. I'll carry it to the car.
Tina: OK. I'll get some food from the kitchen and meet you outside.

B Complete these sentences about Tina's trip with *a*, *an*, or *some*.

1. Tina is bringing ....*some*.... fruit.
2. She's not bringing .... apple.
3. Tina has .... jewelry.
4. She's bringing .... necklace and
   .... bracelet.
5. She has .... credit card.
6. She has .... luggage.
7. She's going to stay in .... apartment.
8. She wants to buy .... furniture in L.A.

C Complete the sentences below with the following non-count nouns.

food	information	music	time
jewelry	money	tea	traffic

1. Tina has a lot of necklaces and bracelets. She has a lot of ....*jewelry*.....
2. There is a lot of .... on the road.
3. Tina's bringing a credit card and some ....
4. Tina's hungry. She's going to buy some ....
5. Tina's thirsty. She's going to drink some ....
6. She needs some .... about her flight.
7. Her plane is late, so she has a lot of .... before her flight.
8. She has her CD player. She's going to listen to some ....

 D Chant

Pretty Woman/Handsome Man

He reads a lot of magazines, but not many books.
He spends a lot of money on how he looks.
She eats fruit for breakfast and sometimes eggs.
She wears short skirts to show off her legs.
He has a lot of credit cards, but doesn't like to use them.
She loves to shop for hats and shoes, and she knows how to choose them.
Sometimes he goes shopping, but doesn't buy a thing.
She wears a lot of jewelry, but not a wedding ring.
She buys a lot of make-up and loves to wear it.
She has a lot of trouble and loves to share it.
He gets a lot of pleasure from the things he enjoys.
Happiness for him is a box of computer toys.

Questions with *How much/How many*

	Count Nouns	Non-Count Nouns
Questions	Use *how many* with plural count nouns.	Use *how much* with non-count nouns.
	How many + noun + *are there*? *How many* + noun + *do/does* + Subject + Verb?	*How much* + noun + *is there*? *How much* + noun + *do/does* + Subject + Verb?
	How many students are there in this class? **How many cups** do we need?	**How much coffee** is there? **How much time** do we have?
Affirmative Answers	Use *a lot of*, *a few*, *many*, and numbers with plural count nouns.	Use *a lot of* and *a little* with non-count nouns. Don't use numbers.
	There are **a lot of students** in this class. We need **a few cups**.	There is **a lot of coffee**. We have **a little time**.
	There are **thirty students** in this class. We need **thirty cups**.	_____ _____
Negative Answers	Use *many* with count nouns.	Use *much* with non-count nouns.
	There aren't **many students** in this class.	There isn't **much coffee**.
	We don't need **many cups**.	We don't have **much time**.
	Use *any* in negative statements with count and non-count nouns.	
	There aren't **any students** in this class. We don't need **any cups**.	There isn't **any coffee**. We don't have **any time**.

A Two students are getting ready for a party for their class. Read the conversation and circle *much* or *many*. Then listen to check your answers.

Lily: Are you ready for the party?

Mike: No, I'm not. How (1. much/many) time do we have before the party?

Lily: We don't have (2. much/many) time. Class begins in fifteen minutes.

Mike: Oh, no! Let's see. I can make the coffee. How (3. much/many) coffee is there?

Lily: I see a whole bag of coffee. There's a lot of coffee.

Mike: Oh, good. Now, how about cups? How (4. much/many) paper cups are there?

Lily: There aren't (5. much/many) cups. How (6. much/many) cups do we need?

Mike: Well, how (7. much/many) students are in our class?

Lily: Thirty. Let's see… there are five cups. We need a lot of cups.

Mike: How (8. much/many) tea is there?

Lily: There isn't any tea.

B Look again at Exercise A. Then complete the following questions with *much* or *many* and forms of *BE* or *DO*. Answer the questions with *any, a lot of, a little, many* or *much*. More than one answer is possible.

1. How ___much___ time ___is___ there before the class starts?
   There _isn't much time before the class starts._

2. How _____ cups _____ there?
   There _____

3. How _____ cups _____ they need?
   They _____

4. How _____ coffee _____ there?
   There _____

5. How _____ tea _____ there?
   There _____

C Write questions with *How much* or *How many* for the answers below.

1. _How many students are there in the class?_
   There are thirty students in the class.

2. _____
   They don't have any ice cream.

3. _____
   There are two students in the classroom right now.

4. _____
   They don't have any sugar.

5. _____
   There are five cups.

D Answer these questions. Write negative and affirmative *true* answers. Then ask a partner these questions. Write sentences about your partner's answers on a separate piece of paper.

1. How much English do you speak every day?
   Answer: _I don't speak much English every day._

2. How many classes are you taking?
   Answer: _____

3. How many people do you know in this class?
   Answer: _____

4. How much free time do you have?
   Answer: _____

LESSON 27

A, An, The, and Some with More Non-Count Nouns

	Singular Count Noun	Plural Count Noun	Non-Count Noun
Use *a*, *an*, or *some* to introduce a noun.	Get a bowl. Get an egg.	Get some eggs.	Get some meat.
Use *the* if there is usually only one.	Turn on the stove. Go to the kitchen.		
Use *the* to talk about the same noun again.	Put oil in the bowl. Crack the egg.	Put the eggs in a pan	Cut the meat.

More Non-Count Nouns

beef	cheese	ketchup	oil	soy sauce
bread	chicken	mayonnaise	pepper	tuna fish
butter	cream	milk	rice	turkey
candy	garlic	mustard	salt	water

Measurement Words

a bag of cookies	a box of cereal	a cup of rice	a loaf of bread
a bottle of ketchup	a can of tuna fish	a jar of mayonnaise	a pound of chicken
a slice of bread	a carton of milk	a teaspoon of oil	a scoop of icecream

A Circle *a, an, the,* or *some* below. Then listen to the cooking show and check your answers.

Good morning everyone! Today I'm going to show you how to make soy sauce beef.

First, you need to get (1. a/the) big bowl.

Then, get (2. a/some) soy sauce. You need about three tablespoons.

Then put (3. a/the) soy sauce in (4. a/the) bowl.

Now peel (5. a/some) garlic and (6. an/the) onion.

Chop up (7. a/the) garlic and (8. an/the) onion and put them in

(9. a/the) bowl with (10. a/the/some) soy sauce.

Now get (11. a/some) meat. Cut (12. a/the) meat into small pieces

and put it in (13. a/the) bowl.

Then get (14. a/some) frying pan and put (15. a/some) oil in it.

Turn on the stove. When (16. an/the) oil is hot, put (17. a/the) meat in (18. a/the) frying pan. Then fry (19. a/the) meat for just a few minutes and your soy sauce beef is ready!

B Here is a recipe for rice. Circle the count nouns. Underline the non-count nouns. Then complete the sentences with *a, the,* or *some*.

1. Get ____some____ rice.

2. Then measure _____cup of rice.

3. Put _____rice in _____pot.

4. Add _____water to _____pot. You need about two cups of water.

5. Add _____salt. You can add _____butter if you want.

6. Turn on the stove. Heat _____rice and _____water.

7. When the water begins to boil, cover _____pot and lower the heat.

8. Wait about twenty minutes. Then uncover _____pot, get _____plate and _____fork and enjoy your rice.

C Tina and her five-year old son, Nicky, are in the kitchen. Nicky is putting away their groceries. Complete the sentences with *a, the,* or *some*.

Tina: Nicky, could you put the groceries away?

Nicky: OK, Mommy. Here's ____a____ carton of milk.

Tina: Put ____the____ milk in the refrigerator.

Nicky: Here's _____bottle of ketchup.

Tina: Could you put _____ketchup in the refrigerator, too?

Nicky: Sure. Here's _____bread. Can I have _____slice of bread now?

Tina: O.K. And then put _____bread on the counter.

Nicky: And here are _____cans of tuna fish.

Tina: Please put them next to _____bread.

Nicky: Oh look! There's _____bag of chocolate chip cookies in here! Can I open it?

Tina: No, Nicky! _____cookies are for my meeting tomorrow. Put them away!

Nicky: Aw… that's not fair!

Tina: I have an idea. How about _____ice cream?

Nicky: Really? What kind do we have?

D Write a measurement phrase in front of each noun. More than one answer is possible. Then put a check ✔ next to the things you have in your kitchen.

✔ 1. _a bottle of_ ketchup

2. _____ soup

3. _____ crackers

4. _____ sugar

5. _____ soy sauce

6. _____ turkey

7. _____ mustard

8. _____ bread

Review

Singular and Plural Nouns
Count and Non-Count Nouns
How much/How many

A **Dictation** Danny is in a bakery. Listen and write what you hear.
Key words: *party, cookies*

Clerk: Can I help you? ....

Danny: ....

Clerk: ....

Danny: ....

See Appendix H for a list of non-count nouns.

B Look at the nouns in the box. Put each one in the correct column. Write *a* or *an* before the count nouns. Write *some* before the non-count nouns. Then add four more nouns.

banana	hot dog	book	newspaper
cheese	sugar	napkin	money
jewelry	traffic	child	apartment
orange	homework	music	furniture

Count Nouns

....

....

....

....

....

....

....

Non-Count Nouns

....

....

....

....

....

....

....

Your Count Nouns

....

....

Your Non-Count Nouns

....

....

C Use words from Exercise B to complete the following sentences. If necessary, make the count nouns plural.

1. The concert is too expensive. I can't go. I don't have any ....

2. I can't go because I have to study. I have a lot of ....

3. The roads will be crowded. There will be a lot of ....

4. I think I'll just listen to some .... on the radio.

5. We can have dinner together. Do you like .... ?

D Complete these conversations. Use *much, many, a lot of,* or *any*. Sometimes there is more than one correct answer.

1. *Two students are talking after class.*

Susan: Do you want to go to the movies with me tonight?

Stan: I can't. Our grammar teacher gave us ....homework.

Susan: How ....homework do you have? I have

...............................time this afternoon. Maybe I can help you!

2. *Two neighbors are talking on the phone.*

Terry: Oh no!

Morgan: What's the matter?

Terry: I'm making a cake but I don't have ....eggs!

Morgan: I'll look in the refrigerator. How ....eggs do you need?

Terry: Three.

Morgan: What else do you need?

Terry: Let me see…Well, I need a round pan, but I don't have one.

Do you have ....round pans?

E A student is looking around her classroom and writing down everything she sees. Write *a, an, the,* or *some* to complete each sentence.

Right now I'm sitting in my classroom. There's ....notebook and ....pen on my desk. ....notebook is black and ....pen is green. There are two students next to me. One is ....man and one is ....woman. ....man's name is Jose and ....woman's name is Maki. Now I'm looking out the window. I see ....old man who is walking down the path. ....man is carrying ....heavy box.

F Write a paragraph about your classroom on a separate piece of paper. Use the paragraph in Exercise E as a model.

Have Fun

A **Tic Tac Toe** Write yes-no questions using the words in the boxes. Then ask your classmates the questions. When a classmate answers "Yes," write his or her first name on the first line. Then ask *How many / much* .... *do you* ....? Write the number on the second line. The first person to get three names and numbers in a straight line, vertical (|), horizontal (—), or diagonal (/) (\), is the winner.

EXAMPLE: A: Do you have any pets?
              B: Yes, I do.
              A: How many pets do you have?
              B: I have one cat.

HAVE ⟶		
pets	money in your wallet	brothers
....	....	....
....	....	....
HAVE ⟶		
pictures in your wallet	American friends	sisters
....	....	....
....	....	....
DRINK ⟶		
coffee in the morning	tea	soda
....	....	....
....	....	....

B Chant

Strange Diet

She eats a lot of eggs for breakfast.
   How many eggs does she eat?
She eats six eggs and a pound of steak.
   Wow! That's a lot of meat!
   Does she put a lot of sugar in her coffee?
She never drinks coffee or tea.
She drinks a lot of lemon juice.
   That doesn't sound good to me.
She drinks a lot of water.
   How much water does she drink?
She drinks a lot, an awful lot,
Five bottles a day, I think.
It sounds a little strange to me,
But she lost a lot of weight.
   How many pounds did she really lose?
She said she lost twenty-eight!

Past Tense of *BE*—Affirmative and Negative Statements

BE in the past tense has two forms: *was* and *were*.
Use *BE* with nouns, adjectives, and prepositional phrases.

	Affirmative Statements	**Negative Statements**
With Nouns:	It was a terrible **trip**.	It wasn't a terrible **trip**.
With Adjectives:	The seats were **comfortable**.	The seats weren't **comfortable**.
With Prepositional Phrases:	We were **on the bus**.	We weren't **on the bus**.

Time Expressions for the past tense:
yesterday/the day before yesterday
yesterday morning/ yesterday afternoon/yesterday evening
last night/last Saturday/last week/last month/last year
two days ago/a week ago/two months ago/five years ago/when I was 16

I was a student last year.
You were late last night.

He wasn't at work yesterday.

Expression:	was/were born	
Correct:	I was born in 1960.	We were born in New York.
Incorrect:	~~I born in 1960.~~	~~We borned in New York.~~

A Teresa is visiting her grandmother Lena in Texas. They're looking at photos and talking about their trip from Mexico to the United States. Listen and write *was, were, wasn't* or *weren't* on the lines.

Lena: Do you remember our trip here? It _____ exactly ten years ago!

Teresa: I remember a little, but I _____ only 10 years old.

Lena: You _____ 10! I think you _____ about 12 years old!

Teresa: No. I _____ 12, Grandma. I _____ born in 1985.

Lena: OK. OK.

Teresa: I remember that it _____ a very long trip. But it _____ exciting.

Lena: Well, it _____ exciting for me. It _____ a very long trip. We _____ on the bus for twenty hours. The weather was bad. And I _____ so worried about our future!

Teresa: But are you happy that we're here now?

Lena: Of course I am.

B Look at the picture and conversation in Exercise A. Complete the sentences with *was, wasn't, were,* and *weren't.*

1. The bus _____was_____ very crowded.

2. The children _____ very noisy.

3. The seats _____ full.

4. The weather _____ good.

5. The trip _____ long, but it _____ very exciting for Teresa.

6. Teresa's grandmother _____ tired.

7. Lena _____ worried about the future, but Teresa _____ worried.

C Teresa and her boyfriend John are at the airport in Texas. Teresa is leaving a message on Lena's answering machine. Read the message. Then rewrite it in the past tense. Change *we* to *they.* Change *I* to *Teresa.*

It's 11:00 p.m. We're still at the airport. It's very crowded and there aren't any places to sit down. The plane is a little late because there's a lot of fog. I'm at a restaurant and John is at a bookstore. We're a little tired, but we're fine.

_____It was 11:00 p.m._____

_____

_____

_____

_____

D Read Teresa's timeline. Then make a timeline for yourself. Explain your timeline to a partner or group.

20 years ago	10 years ago	Last year	Yesterday	3 hours ago
I was born in Mexico.	I was an elementary school student.	I was in college.	I was at my grandmother's house.	I was hungry.

.... years ago	.... years ago	Last year	Yesterday	3 hours ago

Past Tense of *BE* in Yes-No and *Wh* Questions

Yes-No Questions	Short Answers	
Was he/she/it there?	Yes, I/he/she was.	No, I/he/she wasn't.
Were you/we/they late?	Yes, we/you/they were.	No, we/you/they weren't.

Wh Questions			Answers
Why	were	you absent?	I was sick.
How	was	the food?	It was delicious.
What	was	the homework?	The homework was Exercise 5.
Where	was	the restaurant?	It was near my house.
When	was	her birthday?	It was on Friday.

Questions with *Who*			
Who (subject)	was*	adjective/noun/place	
Who	was	absent?	Cindy was absent.
Who	was	in town?	Her parents were in town.

*Use the singular form of the verb in questions with *Who*.

Questions with *was/were born*

Yes-No Question –	**Were you born** in 1990?	**Was he born** in 1990?
Wh Question–	When **were you born**?	Where **were you born**?

A Leo and Cindy are walking to class together. Write *was* or *were* on the lines. Then listen to check your answers.

Leo: What .... the homework on Friday?

Cindy: I don't know. I .... absent. .... you absent, too?

Leo: Yes, I .... really sick. I had a bad cold. We .... all sick.

Cindy: .... your children sick, too?

Leo: Yes. Even my cat .... sick! So why .... you absent?

Cindy: My parents .... in town.

Leo: Why .... they here?

Cindy: They .... here because my sister had a baby. I have a niece!

Leo: Congratulations! When .... she born?

Cindy: Last week. We went out to dinner to celebrate.

Leo: Where did you go?

Cindy: We went to Jo's Restaurant.

Leo: Is that the restaurant on College Avenue?

Cindy: It .... on College Avenue. Now it's on Green Street.

Leo: How .... the restaurant? .... the food good?

Cindy: Yes, it was. It .... delicious, but the service .... a little slow.
        Hmmm. What time is it? I don't see any other students.

Leo: Oh, that's right! It's a holiday. I forgot!

B Change these statements to yes-no questions. Then use the information in Exercise A to answer the questions. Use subject pronouns in your answers.

1. Leo was absent.

   Q: ___Was Leo absent?___   A: ___Yes, he was.___

2. Leo and Cindy were absent.

   Q: _____   A: _____

3. Cindy was sick.

   Q: _____   A: _____

4. Leo's children were sick.

   Q: _____   A: _____

5. The food at Jo's was delicious.

   Q: _____   A: _____

C Write *Wh* questions for these answers. The important information is underlined. Use the information from Exercise A.

1. Question: ___When was Cindy absent?___

   Answer: She was absent <u>on Friday</u>.

2. Question: _____

   Answer: They were in town <u>because her sister had a baby</u>.

3. Question: _____

   Answer: The restaurant was <u>on College Avenue</u>.

4. Question: _____

   Answer: The restaurant was <u>wonderful</u>.

D Chant

AUDIO

Wedding Party

Were you at the wedding?
  Yes, I was.
Was my ex-husband there?
  Yes, he was.
Who was he with?
  He was with Joan.
Who were you with?
  I was alone.
Was the groom nervous?
  Yes he was.

Was the bride in white?
  Yes, she was.
Where was the reception?
  It was in a hotel.
How was the food?
  It was served very well.
The champagne was pink,
The flowers were white,
The band was great,
We danced all night.

Statements and Questions with *There was/There were* + Count/Non-Count Nouns

	Count Nouns	**Non-Count Nouns**
Affirmative Statements	Use *There was/There were*. There was a lake near the town. There were beautiful mountains there.	Use *There was*. There was a lot of traffic. - - - - - - - - - - - - - - - - - - -
Negative Statements	Use *There weren't any* or *There weren't many/a lot of*. (Don't use *There wasn't*.) There weren't any jobs. There weren't many/a lot of cars.	Use *There wasn't any* or *There wasn't a lot of*. There wasn't any traffic. There wasn't a lot of traffic.

Yes-No Questions and Short Answers	Use *Was there/Were there*.
	
	Was there a lake near the town?
	   Yes, there was. No, there wasn't.
	Were there any mountains?
	   Yes, there were. No, there weren't.
		Use *Was there*.
		
		Was there any pollution?
		   Yes, there was. No, there wasn't.
		- - - - - - - - - - - - - - - - - - -

***Wh* Questions**	How many people were there?	How much traffic was there?

A Complete the questions with *Was there* or *Were there*. Then listen to David talk about his hometown twenty years ago. Check *yes* or *no* to answer the questions.

<table>
<tr><td></td><td></td><td>**Yes**</td><td>**No**</td></tr>
<tr><td>1.</td><td><u>Was there</u> a lot of traffic?</td><td></td><td>✔</td></tr>
<tr><td>2.</td><td>_____ any pollution?</td><td></td><td></td></tr>
<tr><td>3.</td><td>_____ a lot of people?</td><td></td><td></td></tr>
<tr><td>4.</td><td>_____ a lot of problems?</td><td></td><td></td></tr>
<tr><td>5.</td><td>_____ a lot of jobs?</td><td></td><td></td></tr>
<tr><td>6.</td><td>_____ a lot of farms?</td><td></td><td></td></tr>
<tr><td>7.</td><td>_____ any stores?</td><td></td><td></td></tr>
</table>

B Look at Exercise A. Write *There was, There wasn't, There were,* or *There weren't* on the lines to make *true* sentences about David's hometown.

Twenty years ago...

1. _____There were_____ many problems in David's hometown.
2. _____ many jobs in his hometown.
3. _____ a lot of people in his hometown.
4. _____ many stores, but _____ always fresh milk from the farm.
5. _____ beautiful mountains near his town.
6. _____ any traffic in his town.
7. _____ any pollution in his town.

C Read these questions. Write your answers in the chart. Then, ask a partner these questions and write his or her answers in the chart.

1. What is the name of your hometown?
2. Were there any stores in your hometown when you were young?
3. Were there a lot of people in your hometown when you were young?
4. Were there a lot of jobs in your hometown?
5. How much traffic was there?
6. Do you miss your hometown?

Your Answers	Your Partner's Answers
1. _____	1. _____
2. _____	2. _____
3. _____	3. _____
4. _____	4. _____
5. _____	5. _____
6. _____	6. _____

Write about your partner.

EXAMPLE:

Sandy is from a small town named Nantos. When she was young, there weren't many stores in her hometown. There weren't a lot of people. There wasn't any traffic. . .

_____

_____

_____

_____

Review

Past Tense of *BE*
There was/There were

A **Dictation** Listen to the story about a crime at a very expensive hotel. Write what you hear. Key words: *guests, Smith, said, delicious, diet*

> *Last night, someone in the kitchen at Hotel Majestic put poison in the*
> *mashed potatoes.*

Quotation marks=
"....."

B A police officer is talking to the chef in the hotel kitchen. Write yes-no and *Wh* questions for the chef's answers in 2 to 7. Fill in the blanks in number 8.

1. Officer: *Were you here last night?*   ?
   Chef: Yes, I was here last night.

2. Officer: _____?
   Chef: Yes, the kitchen was busy.

3. Officer: _____?
   Chef: Two assistants and a dishwasher were here.

4. Officer: _____?
   Chef: The bottle of poison was on the stove, next to the salt.

5. Officer: _____?
   Chef: Yes, I was sick last night.

6. Officer: _____?
   Chef: I was sick because I tasted the potatoes. I always taste my food.

7. Officer: _____?
   Chef: It was delicious.

8. Who do you think poisoned the potatoes?
   I think it _____ _____. (She) (He)
             (was/were)   (name a person)
   wants my job!

C **Find Someone Who** Find out about where and when your classmates were born. First, write the questions on the left. Then walk around and ask your classmates your questions. Try to get one or two names for each question.

When students say, "Yes, I was," write their first names on the right.

When they say, "No, I wasn't," don't write their names. Just say, "OK. Thank you."

Were you born ...	First Names
...in the western hemisphere (North, Central, or South America)	
Were you born in the western hemisphere?	
...in Asia, Africa, or Europe	
...at home	
...in a hospital	
...on the 10th of the month	
...on a Saturday	
...in April	
...in the morning	
...in the afternoon	
...at night	

D On a separate piece of paper, write ten sentences about where and when your classmates were born.

EXAMPLE: *Kim and Denise were born in Asia. Kim was born in a hospital on a Saturday.*

Have Fun

A *Find Someone Who* **Bingo** Use the words on the bingo card below to make yes-no questions. Walk around the classroom and ask your questions. When a student says, "Yes, I was" or "Yes, we were," write his or her first name in the box. The first person to get five names in a straight line, vertical (|), horizontal (—), or diagonal (/) (\), is the winner.

EXAMPLE: *Were you at home last night?*   *No, I wasn't.*

                   Were you and your friends noisy
                   when you were children?   *Yes, we were.*

Were you

…at home last night	…busy the day before yesterday	…in this country two years ago	…born in the 20th century	…a good student in elementary school
…lazy last weekend	…nervous on the first day of school	…married ten years ago	…(you and your family) together on your last birthday	…tired last night
…a happy child	…(you and your classmates) at school five minutes ago	**Free Space**	…a good sister/ brother when you were a child	…shy when you were 12 years old
…born in a big city	…home at 6 o'clock last night	…in the kitchen at 6 o'clock last night	…at work last week	…athletic when you were a child
…(you and your friends) noisy when you were children	…in an airplane in the last ten years	…at a party last month	…(you and your dog) on a walk any time this week	…at the movies in the last six months

B Bring in three newspaper or magazine pictures of people in different places. Look for people who are alone and people who are with others. Take turns showing the pictures to a group or to your class. Talk about *where* the people were and *how* they were. Use past time expressions. See Appendix E for a list. Use your imagination.

EXAMPLE: *They were on an airplane yesterday.*
She was tired.

C Chant

Cheap Hotel

The hotel was cheap,
But it wasn't very nice.
The rooms were tiny,
But it was a good price.
    How was the food?
The food was okay.
    Was there room service?
Only during the day.
    How was the weather?
It was very hot.
    Were there many tourists?
Not a lot.
    How was the service?
Very slow.
    Were you glad to leave?
Yes and no.

LESSON 31

Past Tense—Affirmative Statements, Spelling, and Pronunciation

Reminder

C = Consonant (b, c, d, f, g, h, j, k, l, m, n, p, q, r, s, t, v, w, x, y, z)

V = Vowel (a, e, i, o, u)

CVC = Consonant + Vowel + Consonant

-ed Spelling Rules	
1. Add *ed or d* to most verbs.	walk-walked dance-danced
2. When a verb has one syllable and ends in CVC, double the last consonant and add *ed*.	stop-stopped
BUT: When a one syllable verb ends in *w, x*, or *y*, don't double the last consonant.	fax-faxed
3. When a verb ends in a C + *y*, drop (don't use) the *y*. Add *ied*.	study-studied
Language Note: Don't add *ed* to verbs after the word *to*. **Correct:** I needed to work. **Incorrect:** I needed to work~~ed~~.	

PRONUNCIATION of *-ed* Endings

Final Sound of Verb	-ed Pronunciation	New Syllable?	Example
voiceless	/t/	no	walk-walked
voiced	/d/	no	learn-learned
/t/ or /d/	/ld/	yes	want-want•ed need-need•ed

 A Liz had a terrible morning. Read about her morning and underline the past tense verbs. Then listen to Liz's story.

    It <u>was</u> a terrible morning. First I <u>missed</u> the bus, so I decided to walk to work. It looked like a beautiful day. But then, it started to rain, and I dropped my purse in a puddle. When I picked it up, a dog splashed water on me! Then, I tried to find a taxi, but there weren't any taxis! Next, I stopped at a coffee shop to dry off. I ordered coffee, but I spilled it on my dress. I called my boss to say that I needed to go home to change my clothes. Yes, it was a terrible morning.

98

B Find the thirteen past tense verbs that end in *-ed* in Exercise A. Write in the following columns the base form, the *–ed* form, and the number of syllables in each verb.

Base form	Number of Syllables	-ed Form	Number of Syllables
1. miss	1	missed	1
2.			
3.			
4.			
5.			
6.			
7.			
8.			
9.			
10.			
11.			
12.			
13.			

C Eva had a good day yesterday. Write the past tense forms of the following verbs. Then use the past tense forms to complete the story below.

call ....   relax ....   study ....

like ....   shop ....   try ....

play ....   stay ....   want ....

Eva had a good day yesterday. She .... in bed until 10:00. After breakfast, she .... for her English test. She .... to play tennis, so she .... her friend Sandra. They .... tennis. Then they .... for some new shoes. Eva .... on a pair of beautiful shoes. She .... the shoes very much, and they weren't too expensive. Then she went home and ....

D Write about how yesterday was for you. Complete the paragraph below.

Yesterday was a very good/bad/busy day. First, I ....
Then, I .... After that, I .... Finally, I
....

LESSON 32

Past Tense—Negative Statements and Irregular Verbs

> Study the past forms of irregular verbs in Appendices A and B.

Past Tense Negative Statements

Did is the past tense form of *do*. It is a helping verb. Use *didn't* (*did not*) + the base form of the verb to make a negative past tense sentence.

Affirmative Statements			Negative Statements			
Subject	**Verb**		**Subject**	**Helping Verb**	**Base Form of Main Verb**	
I	watched	TV.	I	didn't	watch	TV.
He	studied	for a test.	He	didn't	study	for a test.

Correct:	He **didn't watch** TV.	He **didn't go** to bed.
Incorrect:	~~He didn't watched TV.~~	~~He didn't went to bed.~~

Irregular Verbs

Regular verbs end in *ed* to make the past tense. Irregular verbs don't end in *ed*.

Base Form	Past Form	Examples	
come	came	He **did** his homework	He **didn't do** his homework.
do	did		
feel	felt		
get	got	They **went** to school.	They **didn't go** to school.
go	went		
have	had		
know	knew	We **took** a test.	We **didn't take** a test.
take	took		

Language Note:
The past form of a verb is the same for all subjects: *I went, you went, he went, we went, they went.*

 A Listen to the information about Jerry. Then read the sentences below and check *T* for *True* or *F* for *False*.

		Yes	No
1.	Jerry went to bed early last night.	✔	
2.	He did his homework.		
3.	He studied for a test.		
4.	He felt good.		
5.	He had a cold.		
6.	He went to school this morning.		
7.	He took a test today.		
8.	He stayed home today.		

B Look again at Exercise A. Write five past tense negative statements about Jerry.

1. *He didn't study for the test.*

2. _____

3. _____

4. _____

5. _____

C Complete the following chart.

Present Tense Affirmative	Present Tense Negative	Past Tense Affirmative	Past Tense Negative
He has a cold today.	He doesn't have a cold.	He had a cold yesterday.	He didn't have a cold yesterday.
I go to bed early every night.	I _____ _____ every night.	I _____ _____ last Friday.	I didn't go to bed early last night.
They take a test every Friday.	They _____ _____ every Friday.	They _____ _____ last Friday.	They _____ _____ last Friday.
She _____ _____ every night.	She doesn't do her homework every night.	She _____ _____ last night.	She _____ _____ last night.

D Read about Susan's life. Underline the present tense verbs. Then rewrite the paragraph in the past tense on a separate piece of paper.

FIRST SENTENCE: *Last year, Susan had a very difficult life...*

> Susan <u>has</u> a very difficult life. She works all day and goes to school at night. She doesn't have much free time.
>
> Every day she gets up very early and goes to work. She works for twelve hours in a factory. Then she goes to school. She doesn't have a car, so she takes a bus to school. She doesn't have time to eat dinner. Sometimes she does her homework on the bus, but she doesn't do her homework every day because the bus is sometimes very crowded.
>
> She has a snack in the school cafeteria. Then she studies English before her class. She is often very tired during her class. Sometimes she gets a ride home after class. She doesn't get home until midnight. Then she goes to bed.

LESSON 33

Past Tense—One Subject with Multiple Verbs, More Irregular Verbs

Twenty-Five Irregular Verbs:

Base Form	Past Form	Base Form	Past Form	Base Form	Past Form
1. buy	bought	10. find	found	18. see	saw
2. choose	chose	11. get	got	19. sleep	slept
3. come	came	12. go	went	20. spend	spent
4. cost	cost	13. hurt	hurt	21. stand	stood
5. do	did	14. meet	met	22. take	took
6. drive	drove	15. read	read	23. think	thought
7. eat	ate	16. run	ran	24. wake	woke
8. fall	fell	17. say	said	25. win	won
9. feel	felt				

One subject with multiple verbs:
A sentence can have one subject with two or more verbs. Connect two verbs using the word *and*.

I **found** the shop **and went** inside.

Connect three or more verbs with commas and the word *and* (verb, verb, *and* verb).

I **came** home, **had** dinner, **and went** to bed.

A Read Fabiola's letter. Write the past tense forms of the verbs in parentheses. Then listen to check your answers.

Dear Advice Column:

Every Saturday I do the same thing. I clean the house or wash clothes. It's a little boring. Last weekend I (want) .... to do something different. I (decide) .... to get a tatoo. I (look) .... up tatoo shops in the phone book and (find) .... one near my house.

I (drive) .... to the tatoo shop and (go) .... inside. I (think) .... about what I wanted. Finally, I (choose) .... a tattoo—a half moon on my arm.

It (hurt) .... a little bit, but it (not, be) .... expensive. It (cost) .... $25.00.

I (come) .... home and (show) .... my tattoo to my children. They (say) .... that they (love) .... the tatoo. Now I have a problem. They want tattoos too!

What should I do?
Thanks, Fabiola

B Write the past tense of these verbs. Then read about Fabiola's daughter, Sandra. Complete the story about Sandra. Use each verb only once.

buy	eat	run ....
come	fall	say ....
go	feel	see ....

Last Saturday started as a normal Saturday. My friends and I .... to the mall. We .... some new clothes and .... a movie. Then we .... some pizza.

In the evening, my mother .... home with a tattoo on her arm. My brother and I were so surprised. We .... , "Mom, we love your tattoo! We want one, too!" But she said, "You are too young." I was so angry that I .... out of the house. I wasn't careful, so I tripped on the stairs and .... down!

My mother .... very bad because I fell down. But maybe now she'll let me have a tattoo!

C Underline the verb in each of the following phrases and write the past tense form of that verb. Then, on a separate piece of paper, use some of the phrases to write a paragraph about your weekend.

<u>buy</u> a car *bought*	go shopping..........................	sleep late..........................
call my family..........................	go to a party..........................	speak English..........................
do homework..........................	go to bed early..........................	stay in bed..........................
eat dinner out..........................	play soccer..........................	watch TV..........................
fix the car..........................	read email..........................	wake up late..........................
have fun..........................	see a movie..........................	visit my family..........................

EXAMPLE: *I had a very easy weekend. On Saturday, I slept late, did my homework, and went to the movies ...*

D Chant

Nice Day

I woke up at six and got out of bed.
I tripped and slipped and bumped
    my head.
I took some aspirin,
Had a cup of tea,
Went back to bed, and slept 'till three.
At three o' clock, I felt OK.

And I said to myself, "Have a nice day."
I picked up my keys and went to
    the store.
But oh! I forgot to lock the front door.
I ran back home. The house was OK.
But I really had a terrible day.

Past Tense—Yes-No and *Wh* Questions

Use *did* with all verbs except *BE* to make a question in the past. *Did* is a helping verb. It is the past tense of *do*.

In questions, always use the base form of the main verb. Do not add *–ed*.

Yes-No Questions				Short Answers	
Helping Verb *DID*	**Subject**	**Base Form of Main Verb**			
Did	he	have	a good job?	Yes, he did.	No, he didn't.
Did	they	meet	on the bus?	Yes, they did.	No they didn't.

Wh Questions					Short Answers
Question Word	**Helping Verb *DID***	**Subject**	**Base Form of Main Verb**		
When	did	you	come	to the U.S.?	Ten years ago.
How	did	you	get	here?	By plane.
How much	did	he	make?		$2.00 an hour.
Why	did	he	come	here?	Because he wanted a good job.
Who	did	he	meet on the bus?		A beautiful girl.

A Listen to Juan's story. After you listen, match the questions and answers.

Questions	Answers
_d_ 1. When was Juan born?	**a.** $2.00 an hour.
.... 2. Where was Juan born?	**b.** By bus.
.... 3. How much money did he make at the brick factory?	**c.** Fourteen years ago.
.... 4. How many days a week did he work?	**d.** In 1975.
	e. Sara.
.... 5. Why did he decide to come to the U.S.?	**f.** Twelve years ago.
.... 6. When did he get to the U.S.?	**g.** In Mexico.
.... 7. How did he get to the U.S.?	**h.** Because he wanted a better job.
.... 8. Who did he meet on the bus?	**i.** Six.
.... 9. When did they get married?	

104

B Change the statements below to yes-no questions. Then listen to Juan's story again and answer the questions.

Statement	Yes-No Question	Short Answer
1. He made bricks.	Did he make bricks?	Yes, he did.
2. He worked on a farm.		
3. He made a lot of money.		
4. He had to get a visa.		
5. He stood in line.		
6. He took a plane to the U.S.		
7. He met Sara on the bus.		
8. They got married.		

C Find the mistakes in these questions. Rewrite each question and then write answers.

Questions	Answers
1. When you begin your English lessons?	
2. Where you lived fifteen years ago?	
3. Were you take a bus to school today?	
4. Did you had a job five years ago?	
5. Where did you went yesterday?	

D Read Juan's timeline. Then make a timeline for yourself on a separate piece of paper. Write at least six sentences about things that happened in your life.

1975	1991	1991-95	1995	1996	1997	2001
I was born.	I left school.	I worked in a factory.	I came to LA.	I began studying English.	I got married.	I became a manager.

Show your timeline to your partner. Ask questions about your partner's timeline.

EXAMPLE: *Where were you born? Why did you...?*

Review
Past Tense

A **Dictation** Annie is talking to her friend, Brad, at school. Write the conversation that you hear. Key words: *really, surprised, once*

Annie: Brad! What's wrong? You look upset.

Brad: ....

Annie: ....

Brad: ....

....

....

Annie: ....

Brad: ....

....

....

exclamation point = !

B Look at Exercise A. Circle all the verbs. Then complete this chart. If a verb is used twice, write it in the chart only once.

Irregular Verbs		Regular Verbs	
Base Form	**Past Form**	**Base Form**	**Past Form**
forget	forgot		

C Complete this chart.

Present Tense Affirmative	Past Tense Affirmative	Past Tense Question
Annie and Brad are good friends.	Annie and Brad were good friends.	Were Annie and Brad good friends?
They spend a lot of time together.		
They meet every day and have lunch in the cafeteria.		
Annie eats dinner at Brad's house twice a week.		
Annie knows Brad's family and feels very comfortable with them.		
Annie and Brad do their homework together and read to each other.		
And every Friday night, they eat out, go to the movies, and have a great time.		

D Write a paragraph about Annie and Brad. Write about the year 1950, and use the past tense affirmative sentences you wrote for Exercise C.

In 1950, Annie and Brad were good friends.

Have Fun

A **Crossword Puzzle** What happened with Annie and Brad? To find out, complete this puzzle with verbs. Use the clues shown below.

Across

4. Annie and Brad .... to college together.

5. They .... married in 1956.

6. They had three girls. They didn't .... any boys.

7. They .... have a lot of money.

8. The didn't .... many vacations.

9. They looked for a house. They didn't .... a nice house for a long time.

Down

1. Annie and Brad .... a house with four bedrooms.

2. Annie .... medicine after she finished college. She wanted to be a doctor.

3. Their house .... a lot of money.

4. They .... happy in their new house.

9. They looked for a good school for their children. They .... one near their new house.

B Spelling Bee Stand in a line. Your teacher will say the base form of a regular or irregular verb. One by one, students will spell the past forms. When students make mistakes, they will sit down. The last student spelling a verb correctly is the winner.

C Chant

They Went for a Walk

They went for a walk, but they didn't go far.
They didn't take a taxi.
They didn't take their car.
They stopped for a while and picked some flowers.
Then they walked and talked for hours and hours.

They went to a coffee shop and drank some tea.
I said hello to them.
They said hello to me.
  Did they have a good time?
Yes, they did.
  Did they go there alone?
No, they brought their kids.
  When did they leave?
They left at three.
I said goodbye to them.
They said goodbye to me.

LESSON 35

Contrast: *BE* and *DO* in Past Tense Negative Statements

See Lesson 28 for a review of "wasn't" and "weren't." See Lesson 32 for a review of "didn't."

Use a negative past form of *BE—wasn't or weren't*—with nouns, adjectives, and prepositional phrases to make a negative sentence in the past:

With Nouns	He **wasn't** a good waiter.
With Adjectives:	We **weren't** happy.
With Prepositional Phrases:	The restaurant **wasn't** in a nice area.
Incorrect:	The food ~~didn't~~ good.

Use the negative past form of *DO—didn't* (or *did not*)—with the base form of ALL other verbs to make a negative sentence in the past. *Do* is a helping verb.

For all verbs	I **didn't like** the restaurant.
except BE:	She **didn't want** a hamburger.
	The food **didn't taste** good.
Incorrect:	~~The food wasn't taste good.~~

A Thomas writes restaurant reviews for a newspaper. Last night he ate at a terrible restaurant. Complete his article with *wasn't, weren't* or *didn't*. Then listen and check your answers.

"Fresh" and "polite" are adjectives.

Restaurant Review by Thomas Lake

Last night, my wife and I went to the Island Café for dinner. It's a new restaurant. It opened three weeks ago.

We (1. didn't/weren't) .... have a good time. It (2. didn't/wasn't) .... a good restaurant, and it (3. didn't/wasn't) .... in a nice area. It was very crowded, and we waited for a table for forty-five minutes.

Our table (4. didn't/wasn't) .... clean, and the flowers (5. didn't/weren't) .... fresh.

Our waiter (6. didn't/wasn't) .... polite. He (7. didn't/wasn't) .... a good waiter. I ordered salmon, but he (8. didn't/wasn't) .... bring me salmon. He brought me chicken. My wife ordered spaghetti, but he (9. didn't/wasn't) .... serve her spaghetti. He served her a hamburger. We (10. didn't/weren't) .... happy.

We waited about half an hour, and he finally brought us the right food. We were very hungry, but the food (11. didn't/wasn't) .... hot and it (12. didn't/wasn't) .... taste good. We (13. didn't/weren't) .... eat it—we paid and left.

My wife and I (14. didn't/weren't) .... like the Island Café. But we were happy after we had some pizza and took a walk on the beach.

110

B Look at the restaurant review in Exercise A and complete this chart with the words that follow *wasn't*, *weren't*, and *didn't*.

	WASN'T/WEREN'T		DIDN'T
With Nouns	With Adjectives	With Prepositional Phrases	With Verbs
a good restaurant	clean		have

C Fill in the blanks with *wasn't, weren't,* or *didn't.*

1. Thomas *didn't* like the restaurant.

2. When Thomas and Erica got to the restaurant, they .... get a table.

3. They waited a long time, so they .... happy.

4. The restaurant .... in a nice part of the city.

5. They .... talk a lot because the restaurant was very noisy.

6. The restaurant .... quiet.

7. The waiter .... know how to do his job.

8. Also, he .... polite.

D Erica is sending an e-mail to her friend. She is talking about her terrible evening at the Island Café. Circle the eight mistakes in her e-mail, and write in the corrections.

Hi Amy,

Tom and I ate at a terrible restaurant last night. We really ~~weren't~~ *didn't* like it. We didn't liked the food—it was cold and it wasn't taste good. And the waiter wasn't bring the right food. When he brought me a hamburger, I said, "I didn't ordered a hamburger! I ordered spaghetti!" He wasn't say, "I'm sorry."

We wasn't eat. We left and drove to a nice area near the beach. We had some pizza and took a walk on the beach. That was fun. The first part of the evening didn't nice, but the second part was great!

I'll call you tonight, Erica.

Contrast: *BE* and *DO* in Past Tense Yes-No and *Wh* Questions

Use a past form of BE—*was or were*—with nouns, adjectives and prepositional phrases to ask a question about the past.

	Yes-No Questions and Answers	***Wh* Questions and Answers**
With Nouns	**Was** she a teacher? Yes, she was.	*How* was Mother's Day?* It was great.
With Adjectives	**Was** she surprised? Yes, she was.	*Why* was she surprised? Because of the present.
With Prepositional Phrases	**Were** you at a restaurant? Yes, we were.	*Where* were you? At Marie's Restaurant.
Incorrect:	~~Did she surprised?~~	~~Why did she surprised?~~

Language Note:
*Answer *How + BE* questions with adjectives.
How was brunch?　　It was **wonderful/great/pretty good/O.K./terrible**.

Use the past form of *DO*—*did*—with ALL other verbs to make a question about the past. *Do* is a helping verb.

	Yes-No Questions and Answers	***Wh* Questions and Answers**
For all verbs except BE:	**Did** you **have** a good time? Yes, we did. **Did** she **have** a hamburger? No, she didn't.	*When* **did** you **go**? On Sunday. *What* **did** she **have**? A salad.
Incorrect:	~~Was she have a good time?~~	~~When was you go?~~

A Yesterday was Mother's Day. Andrew took his mother, Margie, out to brunch. Now Andrew's friend, Rose, is asking him questions. Listen and circle the correct answers to the questions.

1. Did Andrew take his mother out to brunch yesterday?　　(Yes, he did.)　　Yes, he was.

2. When did they have brunch?　　Last week.　　Yesterday.

3. How was brunch?　　It was great.　　It was OK.

4. Did they have a nice time?　　Yes, they did.　　Yes, they were.

5. Where did they eat?　　In Andrew's neighborhood.　　In Margie's neighborhood.

6. Was Margie happy?　　Yes, she did.　　Yes, she was.

7. Did Andrew give her a ring?　　No, he didn't.　　No, he wasn't.

8. What did Andrew give his mother?　　A bracelet.　　A necklace.

B Margie is telling her friend Marta about brunch. Write *was*, *were*, or *did* on the lines.

Marta: Hi, Margie. How (1.) ___was___ Mother's Day?

Margie: It (2.) _____ very nice.

Marta: What (3.) _____ you do?

Margie: I went to brunch with my son.

Marta: (4.) _____ you have a good time?

Margie: Yes, I (5.) _____.

Marta: Where (6.) _____ you go?

Margie: To a restaurant in his neighborhood. It (7.) _____ a great place.

Marta: (8.) _____ he give you that beautiful necklace?

Margie: Yes, he (9.) _____. How (10.) _____ you know?

Marta: Because he called and asked me for advice about a present for you!

C Read the paragraph. Then unscramble the words below to write *Wh* questions about the paragraph. Answer the questions.

Last Saturday, Ellen took her mother-in-law, Annette, out to lunch for her birthday. They went to a nice restaurant at the mall. Everything was delicious. They talked about Ellen's husband, Bill, and their three kids. They also talked about Annette's retirement party. They had a good time together.

1. take/lunch/to/When/Ellen/did/Annette
Q: *When did Ellen take Annette to lunch?*
A: *She took her to lunch last Saturday.*

2. restaurant/was/How/the
Q: _____
A: _____

3. restaurant/was/Where/the
Q: _____
A: _____

4. fun/Did/have/they
Q: _____
A: _____

5. about/talk/they/What/did
Q: _____
A: _____

D Ask a partner five *Wh* questions about his or her last birthday. Then write sentences about your partner's birthday.

EXAMPLE: *How was your last birthday, Pedro?*
        1. Pedro's last birthday was exciting.

LESSON 37

Contrast: *BE* and *DO* in Present and Past Tenses—Statements and Questions

	BE in Present and Present Continuous Tenses	*DO* (Helping Verb) + Other Verbs in Present Tense
Affirmative:	He **is** on the floor. His mother **is** help**ing** him.	——— ———
Negative:	His arm **isn't** broken. He **isn't** cry**ing**.	His arm **doesn't hurt**.
Yes-No Question:	**Are** his mother and brother worried? **Are** they help**ing** him?	**Does** his leg **hurt**?
***Wh* Question:**	Where **is** his mother? How **are** they help**ing** him?	What **do** they **want** to do?
	***BE* in Past Tense**	*DO* (Helping Verb) + Other Verbs in Past Tense
Affirmative:	He **was** on the floor.	———
Negative:	His arm **wasn't** broken.	His arm **didn't hurt**.
Yes-No Question:	**Were** they worried?	**Did** his leg **hurt**?
***Wh* Question:**	Where **were** his mother and brother?	What **did** they **want** to do?

A Adam broke his leg. Look at the pictures and read the questions below. Then listen to Adam's story and circle the correct answers.

1. When did Adam fall down?   Last month.   (Two months ago.)
2. Did he break his right leg or his left leg?   His right leg.   His left leg.
3. Was he in a hurry?   Yes, he was.   No, he wasn't.
4. Did his leg hurt?   Yes, it did.   No, it didn't.
5. Where is he now?   In front of his school.   In front of his house.
6. Is he better now?   Yes, he is.   No, he isn't.
7. Does his leg hurt now?   Yes, it does.   No, it doesn't.
8. Does his brother drive him to school?   Yes, he does.   No, he doesn't.

B These sentences are not correct. Look at Exercise A to find the correct information. Write two sentences for each with the correct information.

1. Adam fell down last week.

   Adam didn't fall down last week. He fell down two months ago.

2. He broke his right leg.

   ....

3. His mother and brother were at the store when he fell down.

   ....

4. Adam is standing in front of his house right now.

   ....

5. Adam takes the bus to school.

   ....

C Write yes-no questions and answers. Then write *Wh* questions.

	Yes-No Questions	Answers
EXAMPLE:	*Did Adam fall down last week?*	*No, he didn't.*
1.	*his right leg?*	
2.	*in a hurry?*	
3.	*better now?*	
4.	*his leg hurt now?*	

	Wh Questions	Answers
EXAMPLE:	*When did Andrew fall down?*	*He fell down two months ago.*
5.	*break?*	*He broke his left leg.*
6.	*in a hurry?*	*Because he was late.*
7.	*standing now?*	*In front of his school.*

 D Chant

Is Carlos married?

Is Carlos married?
    Yes, he is.
Who did he marry?
    He married Liz.
Was Liz his neighbor?
    Yes, she was.
Does she speak English?
    Yes, she does.

When did they get married?
    They got married in June,
    and went to Colorado
    for their honeymoon.
Do they live there now?
    Yes, they do.
She likes it there and he does too.

Review

Contrast *BE* and *DO* in the Past Tense

A **Dictation** Listen to Elena's story about her bad day at work. Write what you hear. Key words: *overslept, mad, crazy*

Yesterday, I had a very bad day because I overslept.

_____

_____

_____

_____

B Write a paragraph about a bad day or a good day that you once had. Write affirmative and negative sentences.

_____, I had a very _____ day because _____

_____

_____

_____

C Complete this chart to make sentences and questions in the past tense.

"Relaxed" is an adjective. It is not a past tense verb.

Affirmative Statement	Negative Statement	Yes-No Question
Elena had a very bad day.	She _didn't have_ a good day.	_Did she have_ a bad day?
She woke up at 8:15.	She _____ at 6:30.	_____ at 8:15?
She was late for work.	She _____ on time.	_____ on time?
She ate lunch.	She _____ breakfast.	_____ breakfast?
Her boss was mad.	Her boss _____ happy.	_____ happy?
When she talked to her boss, she was nervous.	When she talked to her boss, she _____ relaxed.	When she talked to her boss, _____ nervous?

D These sentences about Ricky and Jerry have the wrong information. Write two sentences for each with the correct information.

Ricky in July

Jerry in August

1. Ricky went on vacation in August.　　*Ricky didn't go on vacation in August.*
   He went on vacation in July.

2. Ricky was on vacation in August.　　..

   ....

3. Jerry went surfing.　　..

   ....

4. Jerry was at a beach.　　..

   ....

5. Jerry and Ricky went on vacation　　..
   together.　　...*separately.*

6. Jerry and Ricky had bad vacations.　　..

   ....

E Find the mistakes. Rewrite the sentences.

1. Elena wasn't lose her glasses.　　*Elena didn't lose her glasses.*

2. Was Elena lose her glasses?　　..

3. Elena didn't lost her glasses.　　..

4. Did Elena lost her glasses?　　..

5. Elena was lose her wallet.　　..

6. Ricky didn't found her wallet.　　..

7. Was Jerry find her wallet?　　..

8. Jerry was find her wallet.　　..

Have Fun

A **Sentence Game** Look at the picture of the family at a picnic *yesterday*. Work with a partner and write *negative* past tense sentences about what didn't happen *yesterday*. Use *didn't, wasn't,* and *weren't*. Write as many sentences as you can in five minutes. The pair of students with the most sentences wins if the verbs in the sentences are used correctly.

Some words and phrases you can use:

- busy
- go swimming
- cook hamburgers
- at home
- angry
- at school
- a bad day
- play basketball
- eat at home
- at work
- go to a restaurant
- tired
- a cold day
- wear jackets
- go to work

EXAMPLE:
They didn't play basketball.

B **Guessing Game** Write three past tense sentences about when you were a child. (Use *was* in one of your sentences and different verbs in the other two sentences.) Write two *true* sentences and one *false* sentence. Read your sentences to a small group or to your class. Your classmates will guess which sentence is *false*.

EXAMPLE:

You:	I **rode** my bike a lot when I was a child.
	I **was** a bad student.
	I **cleaned** my room every day.
Your classmate:	You weren't a bad student. You were a good student.
You:	No, I was a bad student.
Another classmate:	You didn't clean your room every day.
You:	That's right! I didn't clean my room every day.

C Chant

No Snow

How was your winter vacation?
    It wasn't fun at all.
What happened? Did you go skiing?
Did you have a terrible fall?

    We wanted to go skiing
    But there wasn't any snow at all.
No snow?
    No snow.
    No snow at all.

How was the weather?
    It rained all day.
What a shame!
How long did you stay?

    We stayed too long.
    Everything went wrong.
    We didn't know
    There wasn't any snow.

Where did you go?
    We went to the mountains,
    But there wasn't any snow.
No snow? Why did you go?
    We wanted to ski,
    but there wasn't any snow.

Didn't you know there wasn't any snow?
    No, of course not, we didn't know.
    We didn't know there wasn't any snow.

Contrast: GO + Activity (___*ing*) vs. GO + Place

Use *go* ___*ing* to talk about an activity. Use *go to* to talk about a place.

Activities	**Places**
go shopping	go to a store, go to a supermarket, go to a mall
go swimming	go to a pool, go to a lake, go to the beach
go camping	go to a campground, go to the mountains
go hiking	go to the mountains
go jogging/running	go to the park
go (water) skiing	go to a lake
go ice skating	go to a skating rink
go bowling	go to a bowling alley
go dancing	go to a club
go sightseeing	go to Hong Kong

Use *go* in different verb tenses:

We **go** shopping every Saturday.　　We**'re going** shopping.　　We **went** shopping.

A Lily and Ron are talking about activities they did when they were young, and activities they do now. Listen and circle what you hear.

Lily: We had a lot of fun when we were young. Do you remember when we went (1. camping/to camping)?

Ron: Of course! It was great. We went (2. to mountains/to the mountains) and stayed in a beautiful campground. I remember we went (3. to hiking/hiking) and (4. to swim/swimming) and had a great time.

Lily: We went (5. to the mountains/to mountains) in the winter, too. We went (6. to ski/skiing) and (7. to ice skating/ice skating). We were very active and athletic when we were young.

Ron: We're still active now. We go (8. to bowling/bowling) every Friday night and we go (9. to dance/dancing) every Saturday night. And on Sundays, we go (10. to park/to the park). That's pretty good for people who are eighty!

B Lily and Ron's granddaughter, Nancy, is on vacation but she is very busy. Look at the pictures and write sentences about where she went and what she did from Sunday to Friday. For number seven, write one sentence each about where she is going, and what she is doing today, Saturday.

Sunday   Monday   Tuesday

Wednesday   Thursday   Friday   Saturday

	Place	**Activity**
1.	On Sunday, she went to the beach.	She went swimming.
2.		
3.		
4.		
5.		
6.		
7.		

C Chant

Where are you going?

Where are you going?
   I'm going swimming.
   I'm going to the pool with Jim.
   Please come too.
I'm going to the zoo.
I'm going to the zoo with Tim.
We went to the pool yesterday.
But it was very crowded,
   So we didn't stay.
I usually go swimming every day,

But I'm going to the zoo today.
I love the zoo.
   I do too
   But I want to go swimming today.
Sally's going shopping.
She loves to go to the mall.
She's going to the mall with Paul.
   I like Paul and I love to go to the mall.
   But I want to go swimming today.

LESSON

39   Verds + Ø, *to*, or *to the* + Places

See appendix A for the Past tense forms of irregular verbs.

You can use certain verbs to talk about places.

come (back)	fly	go (back)	ride	walk
drive	follow somebody	get *	run	

* get to = arrive

These verbs can be followed by a place, *to* + a place, or *to the* + a place.

A Place	*To* + A Place	*To the* + A Place
here	to my house	to the doctor
there	to bed	to the store
inside	to school	to the park
outside	to work	to the zoo
upstairs	to church	to the beach
downstairs	to Miami (a city)	to the mall
uptown	to California (a state)	to the movies
downtown	to Canada (a country)	to the bank
home		to the mountains
everywhere		to the United States*
nowhere		*The United States is a country, but use 'the.'

Language Notes:
Use *come* when you are at the place you are talking about.
(the person speaking is at home): Can you **come** to my house tomorrow?
Use *go* when you are not at the place you are talking about.
(the person speaking is at home): Do you want to **go** to the movies tomorrow?

A Antonio and Julia are famous actors. They are giving an interview on TV. Fill in the blanks with *to, to the,* or Ø when nothing is necessary. Then listen and check your answers.

Interviewer:	Do reporters and photographers follow you a lot?
Antonio:	Yes, all the time. They follow us 1. ___*to the*___ to the store, they fol-
	low us 2. _____ movies, they follow us 3. _____ home.
	They follow us 4. _____ everywhere.
Julia:	Last month we took a trip. We went 5. _____ Spain. We went
	6. _____ mountains and we went 7. _____ beach. But
	there were always people with cameras.
Interviewer:	Did you ask them to go away?
Julia:	Yes, but they didn't listen. And when we got 8. _____ home,
	there were reporters in front of our house. I cried.

Antonio: I remember. You ran 9. _____ upstairs and went 10. _____

                  bed. But I went 11. _____ outside and talked to the reporters.

Interviewer: Why?

Antonio: Well, because I like being famous, and I like to see my picture in

                  magazines.

B Fill in the blanks in the following sentences about Antonio and Julia with a verb, a verb + *to*, or a verb + *to the*. Use the present, present continuous, or past tenses.

1. Last night, a reporter (follow) ___followed___ them home.

2. They get up very early every morning, so they (go) _____

   bed at 8 o'clock.

3. Julia (not/come) _____ United States when she was an

   adult. She (come) _____ here when she was a child.

4. Antonio wants to exercise. He (run) _____ upstairs and

   downstairs twenty times every day.

5. They often (get) _____ home very late.

6. Last winter, they went skiing. They (not/drive) _____

   mountains. They (fly) _____ mountains in their own

   plane.

7. When they were on vacation, they (go) _____ beach a lot.

8. Right now, they (walk) _____ park with their children.

   Photographers are taking pictures.

C Write *true* affirmative and negative sentences about yourself, your friends and family, your classmates, or your teacher. Try to write sentences in the present, past and future tenses.

EXAMPLE: I came to the United States two years ago.

1. (come)   _____

2. (go)   _____

3. (walk)   _____

4. (run)   _____

5. (drive)   _____

6. (fly)   _____

7. (ride)   _____

8. (follow)   _____

9. (get to)   _____

LESSON
40

Verbs + Prepositions

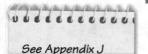

See Appendix J for Phrases with Prepositions.

Use prepositions after some verbs. Put nouns after prepositions. *To, about, of, for, at,* and *in* are prepositions.

listen **to**	She **is listening to** a CD.
talk **to** (a person)	Amanda **talked to** Molly yesterday.
talk **about** (a person or thing)	Davy **is talking about** his day.
talk **to** (a person) about	Davy **talked to** his mother **about** his day.
take care **of**	He **takes care of** my dog sometimes.
wait **for**	They **are waiting for** their mother.
look **at**	He **is looking at** the pictures.
look **for**	I **am looking for** my keys.
ask (a person) **for** something	He **asked** (me) **for** some cookies.
ask (a person) **about**	She **is asking** (them) **about** their day.
arrive **in** (a city or country)	We **arrived in** the U.S. last year.
arrive **at** (other places)	We **arrived at** the airport early.

Language Notes

Don't use *to* after *visit, tell, call,* or *ask*:

We visited ~~to~~ our grandparents.   She called ~~to~~ her mother.

They told ~~to~~ him to hurry.   He asked ~~to~~ me for some cookies.

A Read about Molly, a sixteen-year-old high school student. Fill in the blanks with prepositions: *at, to, about, for, of,* or Ø (no preposition). Then listen and check your answers.

Hi, I'm Molly. Every afternoon, I babysit Amanda (she's eight) and Davy (he's five). Every day after school, I pick up Amanda and Davy from their school. They wait 1. ___for___ me in the school yard. Then we walk to their house and I take care 2. _____ them until 6:00. Their mom comes home at 6:00. She's a single parent and she needs my help.

When we get to their house, the kids always ask 3. _____ me 4. _____ a snack. I give them each two cookies and a glass of milk. Their mom calls 5. _____ them at 3:30 and they talk 6. _____ their day. Davy always wants to talk 7. _____ her first, so Amanda has to wait.

Davy usually brings home some pictures. Amanda and I look 8. _____ them and we ask Davy a lot of questions about his pictures and about his day. Then Amanda talks 9. _____ her day at school and we listen 10. _____ her.

I like my job a lot, and I'm saving money for college. And the kids are great. I really like them.

124

B It's Saturday morning and the children's mom, Lynn, is talking to them. Fill in the blanks with *at, to, about, for, of*, or Ø (no preposition).

1. Lynn: Amanda, look ____at____ your room!

   Amanda: I know, Mommy. I'm sorry.

   Lynn: Do you need help cleaning it?

   Amanda: Uh-huh.

   Lynn: Then you need to ask _____ me _____ help.

2. Lynn: Amanda, what are you doing?

   Amanda: I'm listening _____ music.

   Lynn: Please turn it off. I need to talk _____ you.

   Amanda: Now?

   Lynn: Yes. We need to talk _____ Davy's birthday party.

3. Lynn: Let's go visit _____ Grandma and Grandpa.

   Amanda: Right now?

   Lynn: Yes. I called _____ them and they invited us to lunch.

4. Lynn: Come on, kids. We're late for lunch.

   Amanda: OK, Mom. Come on, Davy.

   Davy: Wait _____ me!

C Answer the questions in the chart. Then ask two classmates the questions. Write their answers in complete sentences.

Question	You	Classmate #1	Classmate #2
1. What kind of music do you like to listen to?	I like to listen to . . .		
2. What do you talk about when you're eating dinner?			
3. Who do you talk to when you have a problem?			
4. What do you usually do when you're waiting for someone?			

Have/Do/Make/Take

Have, do, make and take are used in many expressions.

Have	Do*	Make	Take	
fun	(my) homework	the bed	a bath	a shower
a good time	the dishes	(my) bed	a bus	a train
breakfast	(my) laundry	a mistake	a nap	a walk
lunch		mistakes	a break	a test
dinner		a phone call	a picture	pictures
a snack		an appointment	turns	care of
		noise		
		breakfast, lunch, dinner		

Language Note
*In these expressions, *DO* is the main verb, not a helping verb.

A Read the paragraphs about Lynn and her children, Amanda and Davy. Fill in the blanks with *have / has, do / does, make / makes* and *take / takes*. Then listen to check your answers.

Lynn, Amanda, and Davy are usually very busy. On weekday mornings, Lynn 1. ___takes___ a shower and then she 2. _____ breakfast. While the kids 3. _____ breakfast, she 4. _____ the beds. Then she 5. _____ the dishes. She 6. _____ good care of her children and her home.

Lynn takes the children to school, and then she 7. _____ the train to work. She 8. _____ a break at 10:00, and at 12:00 she 9. _____ lunch. Then she 10. _____ a walk in the park.

In the afternoon, Molly, the babysitter, picks Amanda and Davy up from school. They walk home. They don't 11. _____ the bus. Davy doesn't 12. _____ a nap after school, but he rests because he's tired. Amanda 13. _____ her homework. When Amanda 14. _____ mistakes, Molly helps her.

In the evening, Lynn 15. _____ dinner. Sometimes Lynn 16. _____ laundry after dinner. Amanda 17. _____ a shower and Davy 18. _____ a bath. After Lynn reads to the children, she 19. _____ the dishes and goes to bed.

126

B Fill in the blanks with forms of *have, do, make,* or *take*. Use the present tense in the first paragraph, the past tense in the second paragraph, and the present continuous tense in the third paragraph.

On some weekends, Amanda and Davy visit their father. They 1. ....*have*........ a good time. On Saturdays, they usually 2. .... a big breakfast. After breakfast, their dad 3. .... their beds and then they get dressed. Sometimes they 4. .... a walk and go to the playground. Amanda (negative) 5. .... homework on weekends.

Two weeks ago, Amanda and Davy visited their father. They 6. .... a lot of fun on Saturday. They went to the park. Davy played in the sand and he 7. .... a lot of noise. When they went home, Davy 8. .... a bath for one hour. He was very tired, so he 9. .... a nap. At 6 o'clock they 10. .... dinner in a restaurant.

Right now they are at their father's house again. Amanda has her camera. She 11. .... pictures of Davy in the yard. Their father 12. .... a phone call, so Davy is quiet. He (negative) 13. .... noise. They 14. .... a great time.

C Write *true* affirmative and negative sentences about yourself in the chart in the present, present continuous, and past tenses.

Expression	Present (Every...)	Present Continuous (Now)	Past (Last.../ Yesterday...)
have lunch			
do my homework			
make dinner			
take a shower			

Review

GO
Verbs and Prepositions
Have/Do/Make/Take

A **Dictation** Listen to Johnny talk about his childhood summers. Write what you hear. Key words: *grandparents, exciting*

<u>Every summer when we were children,</u>

_____

_____

_____

_____

_____

_____

_____

B Write the paragraph from Exercise A again, but change it to the present tense.

<u>Every summer, my sister and I visit our grandparents in the country.</u>

_____

_____

_____

_____

_____

_____

C Look at the pictures of Diana and Johnny from Exercise A. Write about what they did when they visited their grandparents. Use the past tense.

They both:

• *went fishing with their grandfather.*

• ....

Diana:

....

Johnny:

....

D Correct the mistakes. Sentences 2 and 7 have two mistakes.

1. Johnny and Diana visited to their grandparents.

2. When they arrived to their grandparents house, they called to their parents.

3. Their grandparents took care them every summer.

4. Johnny listened music every day.

5. Diana told to her grandmother that she loved her.

6. The children talked their parents every Sunday.

7. They went to beach and went to swimming almost every day.

8. They didn't go school in July or August.

9. They went to home at the end of August.

Have Fun

A **Phrase Search** Write the missing words on the lines. Then circle the phrases (groups of words) in the puzzle. The phrases can be vertical (|) or horizontal (—). They can also be backwards.

1. go <u>to the</u> the doctor
2. go _____ bed
3. listen _____ music
4. arrive _____ Chicago
5. talk _____ my friend
6. take care _____ her
7. wait _____ me

8. look _____ me
9. ask _____ help
10. _____ homework
11. _____ fun
12. _____ a break
13. _____ lunch
14. _____ noise

```
R  L  T  X  U  C  H  L  C  R  O  W  N  W  U
O  I  S  T  D  O  A  T  I  E  Y  Z  C  E  K
T  W  V  A  W  Q  S  G  S  H  R  M  T  M  G
C  B  E  K  A  K  K  P  U  F  Z  A  C  T  E
O  D  N  E  I  R  F  Y  M  O  T  K  L  A  T
D  N  Z  A  T  O  O  G  O  E  R  E  Q  K  D
E  J  K  B  F  W  R  K  T  R  D  N  P  O  H
H  B  K  R  O  E  H  C  N  A  E  O  Z  O  C
T  M  W  E  R  M  E  E  E  C  B  I  S  L  N
O  R  T  A  M  O  L  G  T  E  O  S  Q  Y  U
T  R  G  K  E  H  P  L  S  K  T  E  U  B  L
O  J  Y  S  W  O  H  T  I  A  O  C  P  L  E
G  F  K  E  J  D  Z  K  L  T  G  Z  H  Z  V
O  G  A  C  I  H  C  N  I  E  V  I  R  R  A
L  R  F  H  E  A  H  A  V  E  F  U  N  I  H
```

B *GO* **Tic-Tac-Toe** Your teacher will put this game on the board. You will be on Team X or Team O. To get an X or an O in a space, your team needs to correctly add *go*, *go to*, or *go to the* to each item. Your team can talk about what to say for up to thirty seconds. Students should take turns giving the answers. The first team to get three X's or O's in a straight line wins. The line can be horizontal (—), vertical (|), or diagonal (/) (\). When you finish the game, play again with words + *go* from Lessons 38 and 39.

shopping	mountains	upstairs
China	home	my house
there	dancing	store

C   **Chant**

Talk

Come inside.
It's hot out there.
Or go to the pool
And sit in a chair.

Talk about the weather.
Talk about your job.
Listen to the gossip about
Betty and Bob.

Take off your jacket.
Take off your boots.
Put on one of your new
Bathing suits.

Take a lesson.
Learn to swim.
Make a date
With your new friend Jim.

Talk to your friends
Larry and Lee.
But please don't talk about me.

LESSON 42

Future Tense with *Be going to*— Statements with Future Time Expressions

Use *be going to* when you want to talk about the future, especially when you are talking about plans and making predictions.

Subject + *BE* (+ not)		Going to	Base Form of Main Verb	
I'm	I'm not	going to	buy	a baby gift.
You're	You're **not**/ You **aren't**	going to	make	a sweater.
She's	She's **not**/She **isn't**	going to	have	a baby.
It's	It's **not**/It **isn't**	going to	be	a great party.
We're	We're **not**/We **aren't**	going to	give	presents.
They're	They're **not**/They **aren't**	going to	build	a crib.

Future Time Expressions: next week, next month, next year, tomorrow, the day after tomorrow, tonight, in three days, in a little while, on Monday, this weekend

Pronunciation: *going to* is often pronounced as *gonna* or *going ta*.
Don't write *gonna* or *going ta*.
Don't say gonna ~~to.~~

A Jenny is pregnant. She's going to have a baby. Her friends are planning a baby shower for her. They are talking about the presents they are going to give. Listen and match the gifts with the correct names.

.... 1. Linda, Marcia, and Fran   **a.** are going to build a crib.

.... 2. Amy   **b.** is going to buy baby clothes.

.... 3. Tina   **c.** is going to make a blanket.

.... 4. Lily and Sam   **d.** are going to get a car seat.

.... 5. Andrea and Andy   **e.** are going to get a stroller.

B Complete the sentences about what Jenny's family is going to do.

1. Kenny ___is going to___ call his parents and Jenny's parents when the baby is born.

2. Kenny's parents _____ call Jenny at the hospital.

3. Jenny's parents _____ visit her in the hospital.

4. Jenny's aunt _____ send a gift.

5. Jenny's sister _____ baby-sit when the baby is older.

C Write negative statements about what Jenny's friends aren't going to do. Look at Exercise A for information. Different answers are possible.

1. Linda, Marcia and Fran ___aren't going to make a blanket.___

2. Amy _____

3. Tina _____

4. Lily and Sam _____

5. Andrea and Andy _____

D Jenny and her husband, Kenny, are talking about plans and making predictions about the future. Fill in the blanks with affirmative and negative forms of *be going to* with the words in parentheses. Then, in groups of four, role-play a conversation between Jenny, Kenny, and Jenny's parents. Talk about these plans and predictions.

1. We (paint) ___are going to paint___ the baby's room yellow next week.

2. We (not/paint) ___aren't going to paint___ the baby's room blue.

3. Our friends, Sam and Lily, (build) _____ a crib.

4. They (not/buy) _____ a crib.

5. We (put) _____ the crib in the corner.

6. We (not/put) _____ the crib next to the window.

7. There (be) _____ a baby shower in two weeks.

8. It (not/be) _____ a surprise shower.

9. It (be) _____ fun.

10. We (have) _____ a great time.

Future Tense with *Be going to*— Yes-No and *Wh* Questions with Short Answers

Use the future tense with *be going to* when you want to ask about future plans.

Yes-No Questions		Short Answers	
BE + Subject	***Going to* + Base Form of Main Verb**	**Affirmative** (no contraction)	**Negative**
Am I Are you Is he Is she Are we Are they	**going to see** him?	Yes, you are. Yes, I am. Yes, he is. Yes, she is. Yes, we are. Yes, they are.	No, you're not./No, you aren't. No, I'm not. / —————— No, he's not./No, he isn't. No, she's not./No, she isn't. No, we're not./No, we aren't. No, they're not./No, they aren't.
Is it	going to start at 8:00?	Yes, it is.	No, it's not./No, it isn't.

Wh Questions			Short Answers
Question Word	***BE* + Subject**	***Going* to + Base Form of Main Verb**	
What Where When Why Who How How long How many (children)	am I are you is she are we are they is he is it are they	**going to do** tomorrow? **going to go?** **going to go?** **going to go?** **going to visit?** **going to get there?** **going to take?** **going to have?**	Visit the new baby. To the hospital. Tomorrow. Because we want to see the baby. Jenny and the new baby. By car. About a half hour. I don't know.

Special WHO Question: Use *Who is (Who's) going to* + verb when you want to know WHO is going to do something. In this sentence, *who* is the subject.

Who is going to visit the new baby?   Her parents are (going to visit the new baby).

A Sam and Lily are talking about visiting Jenny, Kenny and their new baby at the hospital. Read the questions. Then listen to the conversation between Sam and Lily. Circle the correct answers to the questions.

1. Did Lily call Jenny?   (Yes, she did.)   No, but she's going to call.

2. When are Sam and Lily going to visit?   Between 4:00 and 7:00.   At 7:00.

3. Is Kenny going to be there?   No, he isn't.   Yes, he is.

4. Why does Kenny need some sleep now?   Because he is tired.   Because he's going to be tired.

5. When is Sam going to call Kenny?   In an hour.   Right now.

B Sam and Lily are visiting Jenny, Kenny and the new baby at the hospital. Sam and Lily are asking Jenny questions. Write yes-no and *Wh* questions for the answers below.

1. Q: _When are you going to go home?_

   A: We're probably going to go home in two days.

2. Q: _____

   A: I'm probably going to stay in the hospital for two days.

3. Q: _____

   A: Yes, Kenny's going to change the baby's diapers!

4. Q: _____

   A: Kenny's going to do the laundry.

5. Q: _____

   A: I'm probably going to go back to work in three months.

6. Q: _____

   A: I'm going to go back to work because we need the money.

C In a small group, ask the questions below. Write students' names on the lines if they are going to do what the question asks about.

1. Who's going to go to the movies this weekend? _____

2. Who's going to go shopping this weekend? _____

3. Who's going to study this weekend? _____

Write two yes-no questions and two *Wh* questions about each question above to ask these students for more information. Then, take turns asking your questions.

EXAMPLES: Are you going to go to the movies on Saturday or Sunday?

Are you going to buy popcorn?

What movie are you going to see?

Where is the movie theater?

LESSON 44

Future Tense with *Will*—Affirmative & Negative Statements

Use *will* to talk about the future. We often use *will* to make a prediction.

Subject	Will	Base Form of Main Verb	
I/You/He/She/It/We/They	will	have	a big family.
	will	be	very happy.

Use contractions with *will* when you are speaking.

I'll/You'll/He'll/She'll/It'll/We'll/They'll

Use *won't (will not)* to make a negative statement.

I/You/He/She/It/We/They	won't have	a small family.
	won't be	rich.

When you are not sure about the future, use *probably* or *think*.

Probably	**OR**	**I think *or* I don't think**
She'll *probably* be tall.		*I think* she'll be tall.
She *probably* won't be tall.		*I don't think* she'll be tall.

A Jenny and Kenny have a baby named Katie. Jenny's parents are visiting. They are making predictions about Katie's future. Read the sentences. Then listen to the conversation and write a check when you hear a prediction.

		Prediction?
1.	Katie will be beautiful.	✔
2.	She'll be tall.	
3.	She'll be healthy.	
4.	She'll look like Jenny.	
5.	She'll look like Kenny.	
6.	She'll have blonde hair.	
7.	She'll love to travel.	
8.	She'll probably speak five languages.	
9.	She'll be a lawyer.	
10.	She'll have a brother or sister next year.	

136

B It's two years later. Katie is two and a half, and she has a baby brother named Jamie. Kenny's parents are visiting and they are making predictions about Jamie. Complete the sentences with the verbs in parentheses + *will* or *won't*.

1. I think Jamie (be) ...._will be_........ very intelligent.

2. He (be) .... tall and handsome.

3. He (not be) .... short.

4. He (not look like) .... his father.

5. I think he (look like) .... his mother.

6. He (play) .... soccer, but he (not play)

.... baseball.

C Write about five years from now. First, write predictions about you and three of your classmates. Then find your classmates and read your predictions to them. Say, "In five years, I think you…" Your classmates might say, "Really? That's interesting! I hope you're right." OR "I hope you're wrong."

Name	will probably...	probably won't...
I	will probably speak English well.	
Classmate 1:		
Classmate 2:		
Classmate 3:		

LESSON 45

Future Tense with *Will*—Yes-No and *Wh* Questions with Short Answers

Use *will* in questions to ask about the future.

Yes-No Questions				Short Answers
Will	you		be home tonight?	**Correct:** Yes, I will. No, I won't.
				Incorrect: Yes, ~~I'll.~~

Wh Questions				Short Answers
Where	will	you	be?	At a party.
Who	will	you	go with?	My friends.
How	will	you	get there?	By bus.
Why	will	you	take the bus?	Because we don't want to walk.
When	will	the party	start?	About 8:00.
What time	will	you	come home?	Around 11:00.

Special WHO Question—Use "*Who will + verb*" when you want to know *WHO* will do something. In these sentences, *who* is the subject.

Who will drive?   **Who will** be there?   **Who will** make dinner?

A Katie and Jamie are asking their mother for permission to go to a party. Listen to the conversation and fill in the blanks with the words you hear.

Katie: Mom, can we go to a party on Saturday night?

Mom: (1.) *Where will* _____ it be?

Katie: At Sara's house.

Mom: (2.) _____ it be?

Katie: I think it'll be around 7:30 or 8:00 to midnight.

Mom: (3.) _____ there?

Jamie: Our friends from school.

Mom: (4.) _____ Sara's parents be home?

Katie: Uh-huh.

Mom: Well, you and Jamie can go, but you need to be home by 11:00.

Jamie: But mom...the party won't be over!

Mom: Midnight is too late. (5.) _____ you get there?

Jamie: We'll take the bus.

Mom: OK. But remember—you need to be home by 11:00!

138

B Write each set of words in the correct order to make a question. Then use your imagination to answer the questions.

1. take/what/you/party/the/will/to   Q: *What will you take to the party?*

   A: *I'll take flowers.*

2. do/party/at/you/what/the/will   Q: ....

   A: ....

3. birthday/be/will/it/a/party   Q: ....

   A: ....

4. be/who/party/the/will/at   Q: ....

   A: ....

5. dinner/eat/you/there/will   Q: ....

   A: ....

6. me/party/to/will/take/you/the   Q: ....

   A: ....

7. home/when/come/will/you   Q: ....

   A: ....

C **Chant**

Party Plans

Who'll be at the party?
   I don't know.
Will Jill be there?
   I think so.
Will you bring Jack?
   Yes, I will.
Will you come with us?
   No, we're riding with Bill.
Will Mary be there?
   I think she will.
   She'll probably come with her boyfriend Phil.
What will you wear?
   A sweater and jeans.
   It's St. Patrick's Day
   We'll all be in green.

Contrast: *Will* and *Be going to*

You can use *will* or *be going to* in different ways to talk about the future.

	Will	**Be going to**
Prediction	We **will** have a good time.	We **are going to** have a good time.
Plan		They **are going to** take the bus.
Offer to do Something	A: The phone is ringing. B: I'**ll** get it. A: Can one of you answer the phone? B: Sure. I **will**.	
Decision Made at the Moment of Speaking	I'**ll** see you tomorrow morning.	

A Katie and her brother, Jamie, are talking at Sara's party. Listen to each of their sentences, and circle *Prediction, Plan, Offer to Help*, or *Decision*.

1. (Prediction)   Plan   Offer to Help   Decision
2. Prediction   Plan   Offer to Help   Decision
3. Prediction   Plan   Offer to Help   Decision
4. Prediction   Plan   Offer to Help   Decision
5. Prediction   Plan   Offer to Help   Decision
6. Prediction   Plan   Offer to Help   Decision
7. Prediction   Plan   Offer to Help   Decision
8. Prediction   Plan   Offer to Help   Decision

B Katie is talking to Sara at the party. Complete the following conversations with *will* or *be going to*. Use contractions when possible. Then write *prediction, plan, offer,* or *decision* on the lines to the left.

offer 1. Sara: The phone is ringing.

   Katie: I 'll _____ get it.

_____ 2. Sara: There are a lot of people here!

   Katie: I know. We _____ have a great time tonight.

_____ 3. Sara: We need more cups.

   Katie: I _____ get some.

_____ 4. Katie: This is a lot of fun. I have an idea. I _____ have a party at my house next month.

   Sara: Great idea!

_____ 5. Sara: This chair is very heavy!

   Katie: Jamie is strong. He _____ carry it.

_____ 6. Sara: My parents _____ come in if we're too noisy.

_____ Katie: Oh no. I _____ turn the music down.

_____ 7. Sara: Andy's mom is on the phone. Can someone tell him?

   Katie: I _____ .

_____ 8. Sara: What are you going to do?

   Katie: I _____ ask Bob to dance.

C With a partner, write predictions about problems with *be going to* on the left. Use your imagination. Write offers to help with *will* on the right.

Problem	Offer to Help with *will*
1. I'm going to be late for the party.	I'll drive you.
2.	
3.	
4.	
5.	

Review
Future Tense—*Will* and *Be going to*

A **Dictation** Listen to the information about Grace and her friend, Gabriela. Write what you hear. Key words: *Korea, Argentina, communicate*

Grace lives in Korea right now.

_____

_____

_____

_____

_____

_____

_____

B Write yes-no and *Wh* questions in the future tense for the following answers about Grace and Gabriela from Exercise A.

1. _What is Grace going to study next year_____?

   English.

2. _____?

   In the U.S.

3. _____?

   Her friend, Gabriela.

4. _____?

   No, Grace isn't going to live in Argentina.

5. _What language_____?

   Only English.

6. _____?

   Because Grace doesn't know Spanish, and Gabriela doesn't know Korean.

7. _____?

   No, they won't always understand each other.

C Write affirmative and negative statements about your future plans with *be going to*. Then make affirmative and negative *predictions* about your plans with *be going to* and *will*.

When?	Plan with *be going to*	Prediction with probably + *be going to* or *will*
this weekend	I'm going to go dancing. I'm not going to stay home.	I'm probably going to have a good time. I'm probably not going to go to bed early. I'll probably stay up late. I probably won't get home early.
this weekend		
next summer		
next year		
in ten years		

D Complete the following dialogs with offers to do something. Use contractions with *will* in numbers 2, 3 and 4. Don't use a contraction in number 5.

1. A: I have a headache.

   B: I'll get you some aspirin.

2. A: I don't remember where I parked!

   B: _____

3. A: I don't know how to use this computer program.

   B: My brother is good with computers. _____

4. A: I think I have a fever. I want to go home, but I don't have a car.

   B: Don't worry. We're leaving now. _____

5. A: Can one of you see who is at the door? I'm feeding the baby.

   B: _____

Have Fun

A **Uh-Oh!** Look at the pictures on the left. Something bad is going to happen. With a partner, make predictions with *going to*. Different predictions are possible. Then, look at the pictures on the right. People are offering to do something. Write what they are saying (use *I'll*) in the empty balloons.

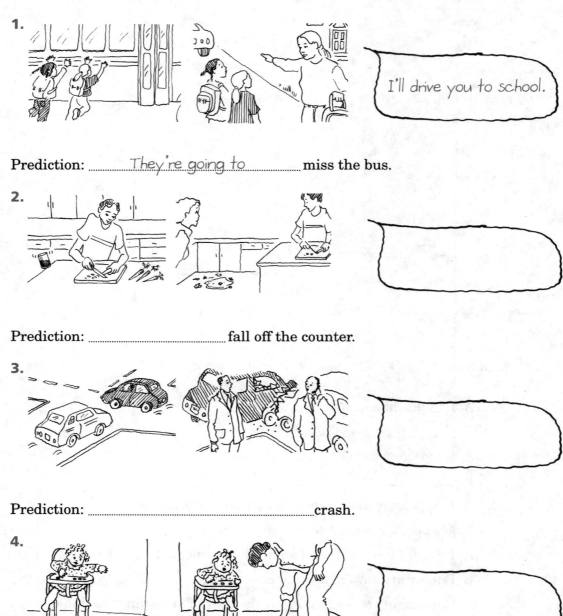

1.

I'll drive you to school.

Prediction: _____*They're going to*_____ miss the bus.

2.

Prediction: _____ fall off the counter.

3.

Prediction: _____crash.

4.

Prediction:_____cry.

B Chant

Driving Lessons

I'm going to learn to drive, but I'm not going to buy a car.
I'll practice every day, but I won't go very far.

     Where are you going to learn to drive?
I'll look for a driving school.
     Will you be a careful driver?
I'll follow every rule.

     Will you stop at all the stoplights?
Of course I'll stop, you'll see.
     The pedestrians will thank you.
They'll probably smile at me.

     Are you going to drive a limo?
No, I'll rent a little car
Of course I'll take you for a ride,
But we won't go very far.

Contrast: *Can* and *Could* for Ability in Affirmative and Negative Statements

Can is a helping verb. Use *can* to talk about ability in the present and future.
    can't = cannot.

Could is also a helping verb. Use *could* to talk about ability in the past.
    couldn't = could not.

	Subject	Can	Base Form of Main Verb
Present	I/you/he/she/we/they	can can't	cook.
Future	I/you/he/she/we/they	can can't	go to the party next week.
Past	I/you/he/she/we/they	could couldn't	read twenty years ago.

Correct:	I **can/could** run fast.	**Incorrect:**	I can/could ~~to~~ run fast. He can/could run~~s~~ fast.

Pronunciation

Can:	I **can** cóok.	I **cán't** cóok.
	(Say *can* fast.)	(Say *can't* strongly.)
Could:	Don't pronounce the 'l' in *could*. The 'l' is silent.	

A Read the sentences about two brothers, Jeff and Martin. Listen and circle *Jeff* or *Martin* for each sentence.

1.	He is a genius.	(Jeff)	Martin
2.	He can run very fast.	Jeff	Martin
3.	He can do complicated math problems in his head.	Jeff	Martin
4.	He couldn't read or write when he was very young.	Jeff	Martin
5.	He can remember everything he reads.	Jeff	Martin
6.	He could read when he was two.	Jeff	Martin
7.	He can't do math problems in his head.	Jeff	Martin
8.	He can't remember everything he reads.	Jeff	Martin
9.	He could write when he was three.	Jeff	Martin
10.	He can play sports very well.	Jeff	Martin
11.	He can't play sports very well.	Jeff	Martin

B Jeff and Martin have two sisters, Kate and Lisa. They're very different. Kate is a singer. Lisa is a chef. Look at the pictures and complete the sentences with *can, can't, could,* or *couldn't.*

1.

Kate _____can_____ sing very well.

Lisa _____can't_____ sing very well.

2.

When Kate was eight, she

_____ sing very well.

3.

Kate _____ sing

tomorrow because she is sick.

4.

Lisa _____ cook delicious food.

Kate _____ cook delicious food.

5.

When Lisa was only ten, she

_____ bake cakes and cookies.

6.

SATURDAY, MARCH 28
LISA-
Martin's Party
9:00pm
KATE- Concert 8:00pm

Next Saturday, Lisa _____ go

to Martin's party, but Kate _____ go.

C Answer each of the questions.

1. What could you do when you were a child that you can't do now?

EXAMPLE: When I was a child, I <u>could run very fast</u>, but I <u>can't run fast</u> now.

When I was a child, I _____,

but I _____ now.

2. What can you do now that you couldn't do when you were a child?

I can _____ now, but I

_____ when I was a child.

D Ask three classmates the questions in Exercise C. Then write sentences about them on a separate piece of paper.

EXAMPLE: When Nooshi was a child, she could run very fast, but she can't run fast now.

Can and *Could* in Yes-No Questions— Asking about Ability in the Past, Present, and Future

Use *can* to ask questions about ability in the present or the future.

Use *could* to ask questions about ability in the past.

	Yes-No Questions			**Short Answers**	
Present:	**Can**	she	walk to work?	Yes, she **can**.	No, she **can't**.
Future:	**Can**	he	visit her?	Yes, he **can**.	No, he **can't**.
Past:	**Could**	you	walk to school when you were a child?	Yes, I **could**.	No, I **couldn't**.

A Lisa lives in New York City. When she was a child, she lived on a farm. Read the following questions. Then listen and write short answers to the questions.

Lisa's Life in New York City

Short Answers

1. Can Lisa walk to work? ......Yes, she can.......

2. Can she take a taxi? ....

3. Can she go to a show tonight? ....

4. Can she have a quiet life? ....

Lisa's Life on a Farm

5. Could she take the subway? ....

6. Could she see stars at night? ....

7. Could she walk to school? ....

8. Could she walk to her friends' houses? ....

9. Could she ride her horse a lot? ....

B Look at the pictures of Lisa's brother Martin. He grew up on the farm with Lisa, and now he lives in Austin, Texas. Complete the following yes-no questions and write short answers.

When Martin was a Child

1.

Q: _Could Martin_ ride a horse on the farm?

A: _Yes, he could._

Today in Austin, Texas

2.

Q: _____ ride a horse to work?

A: _____

3.

Q: _____ drive to school?

A: _____

4.

Q: _____ drive to the gym?

A: _____

5.

Q: _____ see Lisa every day?

A: _____

6.

Q: _____ see Lisa in New York?

A: _____

C Complete the questions below and then interview a partner. Write his or her answers on a separate piece of paper. Then tell a different classmate about your partner.

EXAMPLE:

You:	*When you were a child, could you swim?*
Your Partner:	*No, I couldn't.*
You:	*When Maya was a child, she couldn't swim.*

1. When you were a child, could you _____?

2. Can you _____ now?

3. Can you _____ next month?

Can and *Could* in Yes-No Questions—Asking for Permission and Making Requests

Use *can* to ask for permission to do something.

Questions			Possible Answers
Helping Verb	**Subject**	**Base Form of Main Verb**	
Can	I/we	use a dictionary during the test?	Yes, you can. No, you can't. Sure.

Use *can* or *could* to make a request.
When you use *could* to make a request, it is <u>not</u> the past tense.

Questions			Possible Answers
Helping Verb	**Subject**	**Base Form of Main Verb**	
Can/Could	you	(please)* give me the handout?	Sure. Here it is. No problem. O.K.
	I	(please) borrow a pen?	

* *Use* please *to be more polite.*

A **Part 1:** It's Thursday. Tomorrow there will be a big test. Listen to the conversation. Then read each question and circle the correct answer.

1. Is the test tomorrow?   Yes, it is.   No, it isn't.
2. Can the students use a dictionary?   Yes, they can.   No, they can't.
3. Can they write in pencil?   Yes, they can.   No, they can't.
4. Can they leave after the test?   Yes, they can.   No, they can't.
5. Is the test going to be easy?   Yes, it is.   No, it isn't.

Part 2 It's Friday. The test will start in five minutes. Joe and May are talking. Listen to their conversation. Then read the sentences and circle *T* for *True* or *F* for *False*.

1.	May is reading her notes.	T	F
2.	May says that Joe can look at her notes.	T	F
3.	Joe studied for six hours.	T	F
4.	Joe can use May's dictionary during the test.	T	F
5.	Joe can go home now.	T	F

B Carla was absent Thursday, so she called her friend about the test and the homework. Complete the *yes-no* questions in the following conversation with *Can* or *Could*, a subject, and the verb in parentheses.

Carla: Hi Yolanda. I was absent today because I had to go to immigration.

(1. give) .... *Can you give* .... me the homework assignment?

Yolanda: There's no homework because we have a test tomorrow. The teacher gave us a review sheet. I'm sorry—I didn't get you one.

Carla: That's OK. (2. stop by) .... to look at it?

Yolanda: Sure. (3. stay) .... and study with me?

Carla: I'd love to. I'll be right there.

Yolanda: Carla... (4. do) .... me a favor? (5. get)

.... some cookies on your way?

Carla: No problem. What kind do you want?

C For each situation, write requests with *Can* or *Could*, a subject, and a verb.

1. I can't hear you. .... *Could you speak* ....louder?

2. You're talking too fast. ....more slowly?

3. I don't know that word. ....that word on the board?

4. I was absent yesterday. ....me the handout?

5. I'm going to be absent tomorrow. ....me the homework?

D Chant

Can we use the swimming pool?

Can we use the swimming pool today at noon?
 Yes, we can.
Can we have a picnic with my old friend June?
 Yes, of course we can.
 We can have a picnic, we can go for a swim,
And I can introduce you to my baby brother Jim.

Can children use the pool?
 Yes, they can.
Can Jim swim?
 Yes, of course he can.
Can we stay in the swimming pool very late?
 No, we can't.
 They close the pool at eight .

Review
Can and *Could*—Ability and Permission

A Dictation Listen to Matt and Linda's conversation. Write what you hear.
Key words: *instruments, thought, sang, begged*

Matt: ....

Linda: ....

Matt: ....

Linda: ....

Matt: ....

Linda: ....

Matt: ....

Linda: ....

Matt: ....

....

B Write yes-no questions for the following answers about Matt and Linda. Use
Can or *Could*.

1. Can Linda play the piano?
    Yes, she can play really well.

2. ....
    No, he can't play the piano.

3. ....
    Yes, he could.

4. ....
    Yes, she can play the guitar.

5. ....
    No, she can't.

6. ....
    No, he couln't.

C It's Saturday, and Christopher's six-year-old daughter, Rosie, is playing with her friend, Eve. Christopher is trying to work, but Rosie keeps interrupting him and asking for permission to do things. Write Rosie's yes-no questions.

1. Rosie: _Can we play outside?_

Christopher: No, Rosie. You can't play outside. It's too cold.

2. Rosie: _____?

Christopher: No. You can't call Mommy. She's on an airplane right now.

3. Rosie: _____?

Christopher: Yes, you can have some milk and cookies.

4. Rosie: _____?

Christopher: OK. You and your friend can watch TV. But for only a half hour!

5. Rosie: _____?

Christopher: Yes, I can read to you. What do you want me to read?

D **Part 1** Look at the first chart. On a separate piece of paper, write four sentences about what Rosie's cousins, Linda and Robert, *can* and *can't* play.

	Play Soccer	**Play Football**	**Play the Piano**	**Play the Guitar**
Bill	yes	no	yes	yes
Linda	yes	no	no	yes
Robert	yes	yes	no	no

EXAMPLE: Bill can play soccer, but he can't play football.
He can play the piano, and he can play the guitar.

Part 2 Look at the second chart. Write three sentences about Bill. Use *can*, *can't*, *could*, and *couldn't*.

Ability	**Bill Now**	**Bill at Age Ten**
drive	yes	no
use a computer	yes	yes
run fast	no	yes
vote	yes	no

EXAMPLE: Bill can drive now, but he couldn't drive when he was ten.

1. _____

_____

2. _____

_____

3. _____

_____

Have Fun

A *Find Someone Who* **TicTacToe** Ask your classmates if they can do the activities below. When a student says yes to a question, write his or her first name in the box. The first person to get three names in a straight line [vertical (|), horizontal (—), or diagonal (/) (\)] is the winner.

EXAMPLE: A: *Can you ride a bike?*   A: *Can you ride a bike?*
            B: *No, I can't.*   B: *Yes, I can.*
            A: *Thanks anyway.*   A: *Great! What's your first name?*
                                           How do you spell it?

ride a bike	use a computer	swim
....	....	....
play the piano	write well in your first language	play volleyball
....	....	....
make an omelet	dance	sing
....	....	....

Now write nine sentences about your classmates on a separate piece of paper.

B **Guessing Game** Write about a member of your family. Write two *true* sentences and one *false* sentence about what this person can do now. Then write two *true* sentences and one *false* sentence about what this person could do when he or she was a child. Read your sentences to a small group. Your classmates will guess the sentences that are *false*.

EXAMPLE:

You:	My brother can speak three languages. He can cook. And he can play the guitar.
Your classmate:	I think he can't cook.
You:	No, he can cook very well.
Another classmate:	I think he can't speak three languages.
You:	That's right! He speaks two languages.

C **Chant**

Language Class

Can you speak Spanish?
    Not very well,
    But I can read and write and I can spell.

Could you understand our teacher and that poem she read?
    I couldn't understand one word she said.

I can say *Hello* in Spanish. I can say *Goodbye*.
But I can't understand a thing. I don't know why.

Can you teach me how to read?
Can you teach me how to spell?
Can you teach me how to speak and understand very well?

    Maybe I can help you. I could teach you how to spell.
    But I'm sorry I can't teach you how to speak very well.

Should in Affirmative and Negative Statements and in *Yes-No* Questions and Short Answers

Use *should* or *shouldn't* to give advice.

I think/ I don't think	Subject	Should	Base Form of Main Verb
(I think) (I don't think)	I/you/he/she/we/they I/you/he/she/we/they	should/shouldn't should	get married. get married.

Yes-No Questions			Short Answers
Should	**Subject**	**Base Form of Main Verb**	
Should	I/you/he/she/we/they	get married?	Yes, you **should**. No, you **shouldn't**.

Pronunciation: The 'l' in *should* is silent.

Language Note: Use *I think* or *I don't think* when you are not sure or when you want to be polite.

A Read the letter to Annie. Annie gives advice in a newspaper. Then read the letter to Unhappy Melanie. Listen and fill in the blanks with *should* or *shouldn't*.

Dear Annie,

    I need your advice. I'm getting married next year. My fiancé, Matt, and I want a small wedding, but my parents want a big wedding. My older sister had a small wedding, so now they want to give me a big party. 1. _____Should_____ I have a big wedding? 2. _____ I listen to my parents?

Unhappy Melanie in Seattle

Dear Unhappy Melanie,

    Your wedding is very special. I think you 3. _____ talk to your parents. They 4. _____ know what you want. You 5. _____ keep your feelings a secret. It's your wedding, so you and your fiancé 6. _____ have the wedding you want. Good luck to you.

Annie

B Do you agree with Melanie or her parents? Give your opinion about what you think Melanie *should* do or what you don't think she *should* do for each of these five issues. Different answers are possible. Start your sentences with *I think* or *I don't think*.

Melanie wants to...	Melanie's parents want her to...
1. have a small wedding.	have a big wedding.
2. wear a simple dress.	wear a fancy wedding gown.
3. have a wedding in a park.	have a wedding in a big hotel.
4. have a rock band.	have an old-fashioned band.
5. invite a few people.	invite a lot of people.

1. I think Melanie should have a small wedding. I don't think she should have a big wedding.

2. _____

3. _____

4. _____

5. _____

C Melanie is asking her fiancé, Matt, for advice. He agrees with Melanie about everything. Write Melanie's questions with *Should I* or *Should we* plus the verb in parentheses. Look at Exercise B to remember how Melanie feels. Write Matt's answers—*Yes, you should. / Yes, we should. / No, you shouldn't. / No, we shouldn't.*

Melanie's Questions	Matt's Answers
1. (talk) _Should I_ talk to my parents?	Yes, you should.
2. (have) _____ a small wedding?	_____
3. (invite) _____ 200 people?	_____
4. (wear) _____ a simple dress?	_____
5. (get) _____ married in a hotel?	_____
6. (hire) _____ a rock band?	_____
7. (marry) _____ you?	_____

Have to/Had to in Affirmative and Negative Statements

Use *have to* to show something is necessary or to give an excuse.

	Subject	Have to	Base Form of Main Verb
Present/Future	I/You/We/They He/She	have to/don't have to has to/doesn't have to	study for my test right now. go to the doctor tomorrow.
Past	I/You/He/She/We/They	had to/didn't have to	work late last night.

Pronunciation: *Have to* sounds like *"hafta"* and *has to* sounds like *"hasta."*

Language Note: *Must* is similar to *have to. Have to* is more common.

A Josephine is a very busy woman. She has seven children, she's taking a computer class, and she works part-time. She often has to give excuses to her teacher, her boss, and her friends. Listen to Josephine give excuses. For each excuse, circle the person she is talking to from the three choices below.

1. (her teacher)   her boss   her friend
2. her teacher   her boss   her friend
3. her teacher   her boss   her friend
4. her teacher   her boss   her friend
5. her teacher   her boss   her friend
6. her teacher   her boss   her friend
7. her teacher   her boss   her friend

B Read the following paragraph about Josephine's seven children. They do a lot of chores in their house. Then complete the sentences below with either *have to* or *has to*.

Josephine's children do a lot of work in their house. Carol takes out the garbage every evening. Andy loads the dishwasher on Mondays, Wednesdays and Fridays, and Becky loads the dishwasher on Tuesdays, Thursdays and Saturdays. Mike feeds the dog every night, and Chris sweeps the kitchen floor. Amy and Phillip water the garden.

1. Carol _____ has to take out the garbage. _____

2. Andy and Becky _____

3. Mike _____

4. Chris _____

5. Amy and Phillip _____

C What *don't* Josephine's children have to do? Use the information from Exercise B to write sentences with *doesn't have to* or *don't have to*. Different answers are possible.

1. Carol _____ doesn't have to wash the dishes. _____

2. Andy and Becky _____

3. Mike _____

4. Chris _____

5. Amy and Phillip _____

D Look at the list of chores below. Use your imagination and think of two more. Then write eight sentences about chores you *had to* do and chores you *didn't have to* do when you were a child. Share your sentences with a partner.

take out the garbage   do the laundry
wash the dishes   water the garden
vacuum   dust the furniture

_____   _____

EXAMPLE: I had to take out the garbage. I didn't have to wash the dishes.

1. _____
2. _____
3. _____
4. _____
5. _____
6. _____
7. _____
8. _____

LESSON 52

Contrast: *Should/Shouldn't* and *Have to/Don't Have to*

Use *should* or *shouldn't* to give advice.

I think you **should** come to the party.
You **shouldn't** stay home. *OR* I don't think you **should** stay home.

Use *have to/has to* or *don't/doesn't have to* when you want to talk about something that is necessary or not necessary.

I **have to** get up early tomorrow.
I **don't have to** go to work on Saturday.

She **has to** do her taxes.
He **doesn't have to** buy a present.

Language Note: Remember to use the base form of the main verb after *should* and *have/has to*.

You should **come**.
She doesn't have to **go** to work.

A Joe is getting ready for bed. He is thinking about what he is going to do tomorrow. Read the sentences and then listen. Circle *T* for *True* and *F* for *False*.

1.	Joe has to get up early tomorrow.	Ⓣ	F
2.	He's going to a party tonight.	T	F
3.	He likes Gina.	T	F
4.	He should get a haircut.	T	F
5.	He should buy a new car.	T	F
6.	He went to the car wash yesterday.	T	F
7.	He has to mail his taxes soon.	T	F
8.	He has to do his laundry.	T	F
9.	He doesn't have to get up at 6:30.	T	F
10.	He's going to get up at 7:30.	T	F

B Read the sentences about Joe. Then complete each sentence with *should, shouldn't, has to,* or *doesn't have to.*

Saturday

1. Joe has to get up early tomorrow. He _____shouldn't_____ stay up late.

2. His car is almost out of gas and the party is twenty miles away. He _____ get gas.

3. He's not going to a birthday party. He _____ buy a birthday present.

4. He wants to dance with Gina. He _____ ask her to dance.

Sunday

5. He isn't going to work today. He _____ get up early.

6. His taxes are due tomorrow. He _____ do his taxes today.

7. His taxes are due tomorrow. He _____ watch TV all day.

8. He wants to talk to Gina. He _____ call her.

C On a separate piece of paper, rewrite the sentences from Exercise B. Tell Joe what he *should, shouldn't, has to,* and *doesn't have to* do. Use *You* instead of *He*.

EXAMPLE: You shouldn't stay up late tonight.

D Chant

Good Advice

You should get a new computer
But you don't have to buy it today.
The library should have computers
And the students should use them every day.

You should learn how to fix your printer
When the paper jams and tears.
You should learn how to fix your computer yourself
So you don't have to pay for repairs.

Review

Should and *Have to*

A **Dictation** Jon has to pick up his cousin, Alex, at the airport tonight. Listen to Jon. Write what you hear. Key words: *cousin, borrow, trip, tour*

My cousin, Alex, is going to arrive at 9:00 tonight.

_____

_____

_____

_____

_____

_____

_____

_____

B Alex doesn't know much English. Give him advice about what he should and shouldn't do to learn English. Talk to a partner and compare your suggestions.

Alex, I think you should...

get a good dictionary.

_____

_____

_____

_____

Alex, I don't think you should...

_____

_____

_____

_____

_____

C Alex started English classes yesterday. Look at his schedule and answer the questions using complete sentences.

Yesterday	Today	Tomorrow
6:30 get up	8:00 get up	8:00 get up
8:00 register for classes	9:00 grammar class	9:00 grammar class
9:00 grammar class	11:00 conversation class	11:00 conversation class
11:00 conversation class	2:30 do homework	12:30 meet Jon for lunch
12:30 buy my books		

1. What time did he have to get up yesterday? He had to get up at 6:30.

2. What did he have to do at 8:00 yesterday? _____

3. What did he have to do at 12:30 yesterday? _____

4. What time does he have to get up today? _____

5. What does he have to do after his grammar class? _____

6. What does he have to do this afternoon? _____

7. What does he have to do tomorrow at 12:30? _____

8. What does he have to do tomorrow morning at 9:00? _____

D Jon is unhappy because he has a cold. He is talking to Alex. Complete the following conversation with *should, shouldn't, have to,* and *don't have to.* (Use *should* two more times and use the other words once each.)

Jon: I feel terrible.

Alex: I think you ___should___ go to bed.

Jon: I can't go to bed. I _____ study . . . I have a test tomorrow.

Alex: But you're sick. You _____ sleep. I'll make you some tea.

Jon: Thanks, Alex, but I don't like tea.

Alex: This tea is special. It's from my mother. She said I _____ drink it when I'm sick.

Jon: You _____ worry about me. I can take medicine. I'll be OK. You _____ take care of me.

Have Fun

A **Role-Play** Imagine that some of your classmates are going to visit your native country very soon. Look at the list below and check (✔) what they need or don't need to bring. Then walk around your classroom and give advice to three students.

EXAMPLE CONVERSATION:

Rika: *Hi Mario. I hear you're going to visit my country. I'm going to give you some advice. You have to take your passport, and you should take an ATM card.*

Mario: *Should I take a raincoat and umbrella?*

Rika: *Yes, you should because it rains in the summer. And I want to ask you for some advice. I'm going to visit your country soon. What should I bring?*

Advice about traveling to ....
country

	Can Bring	Can't Bring	Should Bring	Shouldn't Bring	Have to Bring	Don't Have to Bring
your passport						
a credit card						
traveler's checks						
cash						
an ATM card						
fruit						
gifts						
summer clothes						
warm winter clothes						
a raincoat and an umbrella						
a hat						
sunscreen						
insect repellent						

164

B Chant

Late For The Party

Do we have to stay and wait for the bus?
I'm afraid we're going to be late.
Do you think we should take a taxi?
We have to be there by eight.

We don't have to call a taxi
And we don't have to worry about the bus.
Remember it's *your* birthday party.
They have to wait for *us*.

53 Verbs + Infinitives

These verbs are followed by an infinitive: *decide, have, like, love, need, plan, try, want.*
An "infinitive" = to + the base form of a verb: *to be, to do, to go, to have.*

I **want to live** in a dorm.   She **needs to make** money.   They **like to have** fun.
We **love to be** together.   Are they **trying to get** jobs?   Did they **decide to go**?
I'm not **planning to live** in an apartment.   He doesn't **have to visit** her.

Use the base form of the verb after *to*.

Correct: She decided **to visit** us.   Did they decide **to go**?
Incorrect: ~~She decided to visited us.~~   ~~Did they decide to went?~~

Pronunciation: **To** is often pronounced **ta**.
          Want to is often pronounced **wanna**.

A Carmen is going to go to college in the fall. A reporter from a local newspaper is interviewing her for an article. Fill in the blanks with verbs + *to* as you listen to their conversation.

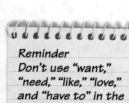

Reminder
Don't use "want," "need," "like," "love," and "have to" in the present continuous tense. These are non-action verbs. See Lesson 23.

Reporter: Congratulations Carmen! You're going to start college in August, but what are you going to do this summer?

Carmen: Well, I have a summer job at a bookstore. I 1. *need to* _____ make some money for college.

Reporter: Are you 2. _____ live in a dorm?

Carmen: Yes. And my best friend and I 3. _____ be roommates.

Reporter: That sounds great.

Carmen: Uh-huh. We both 4. _____ have a good time, but we also 5. _____ be good students. I 6. _____ get good grades so I can go to law school.

Reporter: Well, I wish you luck! ... Uh, I see here that the university is a hundred miles away. Do you think you're going to miss your family a lot?

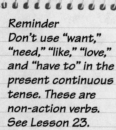

Carmen: Oh, yes! I'm going to 7. _____ visit them once a month. I 8. _____ be with my family. And I'm 9. _____ e-mail my sister every day because we're so close.

Reporter: That sounds like a good plan. It was great talking to you. Good luck in school.

Carmen: Thanks a lot.

B In items 2–4 below, use the information from Exercise A to answer the questions in complete sentences. In items 5–7, write questions for the answers.

1. Q: Why does Carmen have a summer job?

   A: *She has a summer job because she needs to make money for college.*

2. Q: Where is she planning to live?

   A: ....

3. Q: What did Carmen and her best friend decide to do?

   A: ....

4. Q: Who is Carmen going to try to visit once a month?

   A: ....

5. Q: *Does* ....

   A: Yes, she wants to go to law school very much.

6. Q: *Why* ....

   A: She has to get good grades because she wants to go to law school.

7. Q: *Who* ....

   A: She loves to be with her family.

C Ask a classmate the questions in the chart below. Then write sentences about your classmate.

EXAMPLE: What do you plan to do on Saturday?   go swimming
   Sentence: Manuel plans to go swimming on Saturday.

Questions for .... *(name)*	Sentences
1. What do you plan to do on Saturday?	
2. What do you like to do in the summer?	
3. What do you love to do on weekends?	
4. What did you have to do last night?	
5. When did you decide to study English?	
6. What are you trying to do now?	
7. Where do you want to go after class?	

Want (to), Would like (to) and Like (to)

Want=Would like

I want and *I would like* have the same meaning. *I would like* is more polite.

I **would like** a hamburger.   I **would like** to have a hamburger.
Meaning: I **want** a hamburger. (now or in the future)

Like ≠ Would Like

I like and *I would like* have different meanings.

I **like** hamburgers.   I **like** to eat hamburgers.
Meaning: I think hamburgers are good. (I always think this; I enjoy hamburgers.)

You can use contractions with subject pronouns + *would*.

I'd, you'd, he'd, she'd, we'd, they'd

(Use '**would**' with names: Sophie **would** like a hamburger.)

Pronunciation Note: The 'l' in *would* is silent.

Like, want, and *would like* can be followed by a noun or an infinitive.

Subject +	Verb +	Noun	Subject +	Verb +	Infinitive	
I	like	hamburgers.	I	like	*to eat*	hamburgers.
She	wants	a hamburger.	She	wants	*to have*	a hamburger.
They	would like	hamburgers.	They	would like	*to have*	hamburgers.

A Nick is at a restaurant with his little daughter, Sophie. They are talking about what to order for lunch. Listen and circle the words you hear.

Nick: Sophie, what do you want to order?
Sophie: I (1. *want*/like/would like) a hamburger.
Nick: You had a hamburger yesterday. How about chicken salad?
Sophie: I (2. want/like/would like) chicken salad, but today I (3. want/like/would like) to have a hamburger. And French fries.
Nick: No fries today, Sophie. You should have a salad. But you can have a hamburger.
Sophie: OK, Daddy. What are you going to have?
Nick: I think I (4. want/like/would like) the chicken salad. Oh, here's the waitress.
Waitress: Hi. Are you ready to order?
Nick: Yes, my daughter (5. want/like/would like) a hamburger.
Waitress: With fries?
Nick: No. She (6. want/like/would like) a small salad. And a lemonade.
Sophie: Oh, good. I (7. want/like/would like) lemonade a lot.
Waitress: I (8. want/like/would like) it, too. And how about you?
Nick: I (9. want/like/would like) the chicken salad and some iced tea.

B Read each sentence on the left. Then choose the sentence on the right that has the same meaning. Write 'a' or 'b' on the lines.

.... **1.** Sophie likes to have lunch with her father.

        a. She enjoys having lunch with him.

        b. She wants to have lunch with him.

.... **2.** Sophie would like to eat in a restaurant every day.

        a. She wants to eat in a restaurant every day.

        b. She likes to eat in restaurants every day.

.... **3.** Nick would like to order healthy food for his daughter.

        a. Nick wants to order healthy food.

        b. Nick likes to order healthy food.

.... **4.** Nick and Sophie like to spend Saturdays together.

        a. They enjoy spending Saturdays together.

        b. They want to spend Saturdays together.

C Find the mistakes. Rewrite the sentences.

1. Sophie like to go out to eat.   *Sophie likes to go out to eat.*

2. Sophie would likes to have a hamburger.

3. Sophie's brother likes to play soccer tomorrow.

4. Philip likes to buy a soccer ball this afternoon.

5. Sophie's big sister, Eileen, would like get a puppy.

6. Sophie likes to have some milk right now.

D Ask two classmates the questions below. Write their names and take short notes.

Name	Notes
	What do you like to do on your birthday every year?
....	....
....	....
	What would you like to do on your next birthday?
....	....
....	....

On a separate piece of paper, write four sentences about your classmates.

EXAMPLE: Ann likes to go out to dinner on her birthday every year. She'd like to go dancing on her next birthday.

Yes-No and *Wh* Questions with Like (*to*) and Would like (*to*)

Do you like (to) ...? means "Do you enjoy . . . ?" or "Do you think ...is good?"

Yes-No Questions	Possible Answers
Do you like tea?	Yes, I do./ Sometimes.
Do you like to drink tea?	No, I don't./ Not really.

Would you like (to) ...? means "Do you want (to)...?"
Use *Would you like (to)* to make an offer or invitation.

An Offer	Possible Answers
Would you like some tea?	Sure./Yes, thank you./Yes, I would.
	No, thank you./Thank you, but not right now.

An Invitation	Possible Answers
Would you like to go out to dinner?	Sure./Yes, that sounds great.
	Thank you, but I can't./I'm sorry, but I can't.

Where/What Questions and Answers

What **do you like to** eat?	I **like** everything — meat, fish, vegetables...
Where **do you like to** go?	I **like to** go to the Chinese restaurant near my house.
Where **would you like to** eat?	How about at a Moroccan restaurant?
What **would you like to** order?	I think **I'd like** the lamb and vegetables.

A Greg is asking Nicole for a date. Listen to the conversation. Fill in the blanks with the words you hear.

Nicole: Hello.

Greg: Hi, Nicole. This is Greg—I'm Jill's brother.

Nicole: Oh, hi, Greg! How are you?

Greg: Pretty good. Uh, I got your number from Jill. I was wondering... _____ have dinner on Friday night?

Nicole: I'm sorry, but I can't Friday night. How about Saturday night?

Greg: Saturday's fine. What _____ eat?

Nicole: I like everything. Mexican, Thai, Vietnamese, Indian, Italian...

Greg: _____ Moroccan food?

Nicole: Yes, I do. I love it!

Greg: Well, there's a really good Moroccan restaurant in the city. They
have great food and music. .... try that?

Nicole: Sure. It sounds great.

Greg: OK. I'll pick you up at 7:00.

Nicole: Perfect. See you on Saturday. Bye.

B Greg and Nicole are on their date. These are some of the questions Greg
asks Nicole. Circle the correct question phrase from those in parentheses.

1. Q: (Would you like to/Do you like to) sit at a regular table or at a low table?
   A: At a low table.

2. Q: (Would you like to/Do you like to) eat out?
   A: Yes, I do.

3. Q: (What would you like to/What do you like to) have?
   A: I think I'll have the lamb and vegetables.

4. Q: (Would you like to/Do you like to) go out again next week?
   A: Yes, I would.

5. Q: (Where would you like to/Where do you like to) go next week?
   A: How about a Thai restaurant?

C Chant

What do you like to do?

I like Mrs. Brown.
   I do too.
I'd like to take her English class.
   I would too.
Do you like photography?
   Yes, I do.
I'd like to take a black and white photo of you.

What do you like to do?
   I like to ski.
Would you like to take a skiing course with me?
   Yes, I would.
   Do you like the sea?
   Would you like to sail to Hawaii with me?
I love the sea
And sailing too
And I'd love to sail to Hawaii with you.

Review
Verbs + Infinitives

A **Dictation** Emily and her friend are at the tourist information office in San Francisco. Martin, who works in the office, is giving them information. Write the conversation that you hear. Key words: *bus tour, you'll*

Martin: Hi. How can I help you?

Emily: ....

Martin: ....

Emily: ....
....

Martin: ....
....

Emily: ....

B Emily is sending her sister a postcard from San Francisco. Correct the errors in the second paragraph.

Hi Andy,

   Greetings from San Francisco! It's beautiful here. You have ^to^ come here someday.

   We decided to took a bus tour this morning because we want see a lot today. Tomorrow we need go to L.A., but I plan come back to San Francisco. I will try find a job because I want move here. I like to live here forever!

   Miss You,

Emily

Andrea Chang
257 Summer Street
Boston, MA 05682

C Complete each of the following questions with *Do you like* or *Would you like*.

1. <u>Would you like</u> to come over and watch a movie?

   Thanks. I'd love to, but I can't tonight.

2. _____ a cup of coffee?

   Thanks. That would be great.

3. _____ some cream and sugar?

   No thanks. I take my coffee black.

4. _____ tea?

   Sometimes. But I usually drink coffee.

5. _____ to cook?

   Sometimes. On the weekends when I have time.

D In the first chart below, write yes-no questions about movies and studying English. In the second chart, write *Wh* questions about TV programs and music. Then ask your partner the questions in the second chart. Take notes and write your partner's answers on a separate piece of paper.

Topics	Do you like (to)...	Would you like to... (invitation)	Would you like... (offer)
Food	<u>Do you like</u> Chinese food?	<u>Would you like to</u> go to a Chinese restaurant?	<u>Would you like</u> some rice?
Movies	_____ movies?	_____ go to the movies?	_____ some popcorn?
Studying English	_____ study English?	_____ study together?	_____ help with your English?

Topics	What ____ do you like to...	What would you like to...
About Food	What <u>do you like to</u> eat for dinner?	What <u>would you like to</u> eat tonight?
TV Programs	What TV programs _____ watch?	What TV program _____ watch right now?
Kinds of Music	What kinds of music _____ listen to?	What kind of music _____ listen to right now?

Have Fun

A *Find Someone Who* **Bingo** Use the words on the bingo card below to make yes-no questions in the present, present continuous, and past tenses. Walk around the classroom and ask your questions. When a student says "Yes," write his or her first name in the box. The first person to get five names in a straight line [vertical (|), horizontal (—), or diagonal (/) (\)] is the winner.

EXAMPLE:
A: *Do you like to go swimming?*
B: *No, I don't.*
A: OK. *Thank you.*

A: *Do you like to go swimming?*
B: *Yes, I do.*
A: *Great! What's your first name? How do you spell it?*

likes to go swimming	would like a cup of coffee	had to work yesterday	needs to study more	is trying hard to learn English
loves to watch TV	wants to have a snack right now	would like to go home now	has to go to work later	needed to go shopping yesterday
tries to speak English every day	likes chocolate ice cream	**Free Space**	wants a cold drink	likes to go to the movies
liked to eat vegetables when she/he was a child	wants to learn English quickly	is planning to take a vacation next summer	likes to listen to music	had to do homework yesterday
would like to buy some new CDs	likes to use the Internet	has to cook dinner tonight or tomorrow night	wants to buy a cell phone	called a friend last week

Now write five sentences about your classmates on a separate piece of paper.

B Bring in three pictures of people from magazines or newspapers. Take turns showing them to a group or to your class. Use your imagination and talk about the people. Use some of the following words.

like to	would like to	need to	are planning to
love to	want to	have to	are trying to

EXAMPLE: These two people love to go skiing.

C Chant

Dreams

I'd like to go to Texas
And learn to ride a horse.
I want to go to Hollywood
And see the stars, of course.

I'd like to live in London.
I like that English tea.
I'd like to leave tomorrow.
Would you like to come with me?

I'd like to move to Tahiti
And live in a house on the sea.
I'd like to leave this afternoon.
Would you like to come with me?

Imperatives (Commands)

Use imperatives to give instructions, make requests, make suggestions, give warnings, and give reminders.

	Affirmative - Base Form of Verb	Negative - Don't + Base Form of Verb
Instructions (Directions):	**Turn off** your cell phones.	**Don't turn** right.
Requests:	Please* **close** the door.	Please **don't smoke** in here.
Suggestions:	**Relax.**	**Don't worry.**
Warnings:	**Watch out!** **Be careful!** **Freeze!**** **Stop!**	**Don't look** at your classmate's test! **Don't move!** **Don't do** that!
Reminders:	**Remember** to call me later.	**Don't forget** your keys.

*Use please *to make requests more polite.*
**Freeze = STOP *and* DON'T MOVE! *Police often say this.*

A A kindergarten class is playing the game "Simon Says." The children have to follow the instructions only when the teacher says "Simon Says." If they follow the instructions when the teacher does *not* say "Simon Says," they have to sit down and stop playing. Listen to the teacher's instructions. Put a check on the line when she says "Simon Says."

	Commands	Simon Says
1.	Close your eyes.	✔
2.	Touch your knees.	....
3.	Touch your toes.	....
4.	Put your right hand on your head.	....
5.	Stand on your left foot.	....
6.	Jump three times.	....
7.	Turn around three times.	....
8.	Clap your hands.	....
9.	Open your mouth.	....
10.	Cover your ears.	....

B Look at the pictures of people at an airport and on a plane. Use the sentences in the box below to write what the people are saying.

Watch out!	Please turn off all electronic equipment.
Please fasten your seatbelt.	Don't worry!

1.

....

2.

....

3.

....

4.

....

C Write four imperative sentences for each situation. You choose a situation for number 4.

Situation	Affirmative	Negative
1. How to learn English:	Go to school.	Don't be shy.
	....	....
2. Things that teachers say:	....	....
	....	....
3. Things that parents say to their children:	....	....
	....	....
4. .... : *(you decide)*	....	....
	....	....

LESSON
57 *Let's*

Use *let's* to suggest that you and someone else do something now or in the future.

Let's go.   **Let's** go to the movies.   **Let's** stay home.   **Let's** take a walk.
Let's go camping. **Let's** ask for information.   **Let's** dance.   **Let's** take a break.

It is common to say, "Let's (do something) and (do something else)":
Let's get up early **and** go swimming.

Possible Answers (when you agree)

OK.   Good idea!   Great idea!

Possible Answers (when you disagree)

Let's not . . .	+	a different suggestion:

Let's not go there.   **Let's** stay here.
Let's not eat out.   **Let's** eat at home.
Let's not go shopping today.   **Let's** go tomorrow.
Let's not drive.   **Let's** walk.

A Triplets Larry, Barry and Harry are camping in Florida. They are making suggestions about what to do, but one of them always disagrees. They will do only the things that *two* of them agree on. Listen to their conversations, and circle what they *will* do from each pair of choices below.

1. They will go swimming.
   They will take a walk.

2. They will eat now.
   They won't eat now.

3. They will go into town.
   They won't go into town.

4. They will make a campfire.
   They won't make a campfire.

5. They will talk to some girls.
   They won't talk to some girls.

B The triplets finished their camping trip. Now they are driving to the beach. They have many ideas about what to do there, and they all agree. Use your imagination and add to their suggestions by filling in the blanks in the following conversations.

1. Harry: Let's call Mom and Dad right away.

   Barry: Good idea. And _let's call Sandy,_ _____ too.

2. Larry: Let's find a good motel.

   Barry: Yeah. And I'm hungry, so _____ too.

3. Barry: Let's go swimming.

   Harry: O.K. And _____ too.

4. Harry: Let's relax on the beach.

   Larry: Great idea. And _____ too.

C The triplets disagree about what to do. Write sentences on the lines about what they can do.

1. Larry: I don't like this motel. Let's go home.

   Barry: _Let's not go home. Let's find a different motel._

2. Harry: Let's go to a fast food restaurant.

   Larry: _____

3. Barry: Let's go dancing tonight.

   Harry: _____

4. Larry: Let's meet at seven o'clock.

   Barry: _____

D Imagine that you are talking to a classmate before and after class. Write suggestions with *Let's* for these situations. Use *Let's not* in number 5.

1. You have a test tomorrow.   _Let's study together tonight._

2. Your classroom is hot.   _____

3. Your classroom is cold.   _____

4. School will end in two weeks.   _____

5. You and your classmate are very sleepy.   _____

6. You and your classmate are hungry.   _____

58

Too and *Very* + Adjectives

Use *too* and *very* before adjectives. *Too* and *very* have different meanings.	
We usually use **too** to talk about a problem that makes it impossible to do something.	You can use **very** just to make an adjective stronger or to introduce a good or bad result.
Too (a problem → a bad result)	**Very (→ a bad or good result)**
The chicken is **too** spicy. I can't eat it.	The chicken is **very** spicy. I can't eat it. (bad) The chicken is **very** spicy, but I like it. (good) He is **very** good-looking.

Language Note: Don't use *too* just to make an adjective stronger.

Correct:　　He's **very** good-looking
Incorrect:　~~He's too good-looking.~~

A Read the following conversations and fill in the blanks with *too* or *very*. Then listen to the conversations to check your answers.

1. Bill: How's your dinner?

   Ruby: The chicken is ____too____ spicy! I can't eat it!

2. Bill: Wow! This chicken is _____ spicy!

   Ruby: Do you want to order something else?

   Bill: No! I love spicy food.

3. Ruby: Why aren't you eating?

   Bill: My soup is _____ hot. I can't eat it right now.

4. Ruby: How was the meeting?

   Bill: It was _____ long, but it was OK.

5. Ruby: I want to go home.

   Bill: Why?

   Ruby: This party is _____ noisy and crowded.

6. Ruby: How's the party?

   Bill: It's _____ noisy and crowded, but I'm having a great time.

7. Ruby: Let's go out to dinner.

   Bill: I'm sorry, I can't. I'm _____ tired. I can't go out.

8. Ruby: Let's go out to dinner.

   Bill: Good idea! I'm _____ tired, and I don't want to cook.

B Complete Bill's and Ruby's sentences with *too* or *very*.

1. Bill: The car is _____too_____ expensive. I can't buy it.
2. Ruby: The sweater is _____ expensive, but I'm going to buy it.
3. Bill: This box is _____ heavy, but I can carry it.
4. Ruby: This box is _____ heavy. I can't carry it. Can you help me?
5. Bill: I couldn't visit Al at the hospital last night. I was _____ busy.
6. Ruby: I was _____ busy, but I visited him.
7. Ruby: This cake is _____ sweet. I can't eat it.
8. Bill: It's _____ sweet, but I like it.
9. Ruby: I loved that movie. It was _____ interesting.
10. Bill: I didn't like it. It was _____ long.

C Complete the sentences with *too* or *very* for each picture.

1.
Bill is _____very_____ tall.

2.
Her shoes are _____ big.

3.
His shirt is _____ small.

4.
Her sweater is _____ long.

5.
The TV is _____ loud.

6.
His book is _____ interesting.

LESSON
59

Too many, Too Much, and *A lot of*

> *See Lesson 25 and Appendix H for information on count and non-count nouns.*

Too many and *too much* mean "more than necessary." There is a bad result.

I ate **too many** cookies. I feel sick.
I drank **too much** coffee. I can't sleep.

A lot of means "a large number or amount." There can be a good or bad result, or no result.

I did **a lot of** work today. I can take the day off tomorrow. *(good)*
I drank **a lot of** coffee. I can't sleep. *(bad)*
I made **a lot of** cookies for the party. *(no result)*

Use *too many* **with plural count nouns.**
Use *too much* **with non-count nouns.**
Use *a lot of* **with both plural count nouns and non-count nouns.**

A Listen to the conversation and fill in the blanks with *too many, too much* or *a lot of.*

Molly: What's wrong?

Alice: I want to move.

Molly: Why?

Alice: It's my roommates. I can't study because there are always

.... people in our apartment. And I can't sleep because

they make .... noise.

Molly: That's terrible.

Alice: And they never clean up. There are always .... dirty

dishes in the sink. And they buy .... junk food—candy

and chips and sodas.

Molly: You need to talk to them! You have .... problems, but

maybe your roommates can try to change.

Alice: I don't think so. I need to find a new apartment.

Molly: Do you want to move in with me?

182

B Molly wants Alice to move in with her. First, circle the count nouns and underline the non-count nouns. Then, complete the sentences with *too many* or *too much*.

Molly says:

1. I don't make ___too much___ noise.

2. I don't have _____ parties.

3. I don't buy _____ junk food.

4. I don't get _____ phone calls.

5. You pay _____ money for rent right now.

6. You have _____ problems with your roommates.

   You should move in with me.

C Alice's roommate is talking about a party at their apartment last night. First, circle the count nouns and underline the non-count nouns. Then, complete the sentences with *too many, too much,* or *a lot of*. More than one answer may be possible.

Last night,

1. I ate ___too many___ cookies at the party. I felt sick.

2. I bought _____ food. We had to throw some away.

3. I spent _____ money. Now I have only $5 until next month.

4. I invited _____ people. It was very crowded, but it was great.

5. I had _____ fun.

6. I danced with _____ people. I love dancing.

7. We didn't use paper plates. Today I have to wash _____ dishes.

D Chant

You brought a lot.

You brought a lot of luggage.
   I need a lot of things.

You packed too much jewelry,
too many rings,
too many credit cards,
too much cash,
too many photos of our old dog Flash,
too many boxes,

too many bags,
too much luggage
with too many tags.

Why did you bring so many bathing
suits to wear?
All you're going to do is sit around in a
   chair.

Review

Imperatives, *Let's*, *Too* and *Very*, *Too Many* and *Too Much*

A **Dictation** Listen to the recipe for scrambled eggs. Write what you hear. Key words: *recipe, pan, beat, fork, add, pour, spoon*

OK. Let's make scrambled eggs!

B Read the sentences on the left. Then write additional sentences with the verb *be* in the present or past tense + *too* or *very*.

		Subject	Present or Past *Be*	Too or *Very*	Adjective
1.	I can't hear you.	*The music*	*is*	*too*	*loud.*
2.	She liked the movie.	*It*	*was*	*very*	*interesting.*
3.	He can't stay awake.	He			sleepy.
4.	I can't sleep at night.	My neighbors			noisy.
5.	He likes the actress.	She			beautiful.
6.	She's 12 years old and she can't drive.	She			young.
7.	I couldn't work last night.	I			tired.
8.	Everyone was wearing a warm jacket yesterday.	It			cold.

C Bonnie has a lot of ideas about going somewhere and having fun. But Bob always says no. Follow the examples in number 1 and write what Bob says to Bonnie. Use *too much* or *too many* in your second sentence.

Bonnie's Ideas (suggestions)	What Bob Says
1. Let's go camping at the river.	No, <u>let's not go camping at the river.</u>
	There (mosquitoes) <u>are too many mosquitoes</u> <u>at the river.</u>
	Let's (camping) <u>go camping in the back yard!</u>
2. Let's go to the city.	No, ...
	There (traffic) ....
	....
	Let's (beach) ....
3. Let's go to that new restaurant.	No, ...
	There (noisy teenagers) ....
	....
	Let's (on a picnic) ....
4. Let's go to L.A. for vacation.	No, ...
	There (pollution) ....
	....
	Let's (*your choice*) ....

D Write a recipe for a kind of food from your native country.

> This is a recipe for ....
>
> **Ingredients:**
> - ....
> - ....
> - ....
> - ....
> - ....
> - ....
>
> **Directions:**
> 1. ....
> 2. ....
> 3. ....
> 4. ....
> 5. ....

Have Fun

A **Communication Gap** Work with a partner. One student will be Student A and the other will be Student B.

Student A: Go to page 211. Read the sentences to Student B. Student B will draw a school as you describe it. Then Student B will describe a house to you while you draw.

Student B: Draw a school in the box below while Student A describes it. Then go to page 213 and read the sentences to Student A.

When you're both finished, compare your drawings with the drawings on pages 211 and 213.

<u>**I am Student**</u>   **A**   **B**

B Chant

I'm too tired.

Let's go out.
It's hot in here.
⠀⠀⠀I'm too tired to go out.

But it's very hot in here.
⠀⠀⠀I know, but I'm too tired to go out.
⠀⠀⠀Open a window.
⠀⠀⠀Turn on the fan.
⠀⠀⠀I'm too tired to go out.

It's hot in here.
⠀⠀⠀I know it is,
⠀⠀⠀But I'm too tired to go out.

Let's walk to the park.
⠀⠀⠀I'm too tired to walk.

Let's take the car.
⠀⠀⠀I'm too tired to drive.

It's very hot in here.
⠀⠀⠀I know, but I'm too tired to go out.

LESSON 60

Comparative Adjectives—Spelling

Use a comparative adjective to compare TWO people, places, or things.

Peter is **tall**. Pierre is **taller**.

	Adjectives	Comparative Adjectives
For one -syllable adjectives: • add *er*	old	older
• add only *r* when the adjective ends in *e*	late	later
• double the final consonant and add *er* when the adjective ends in CVC (consonant + vowel + consonant)	big	bi**gg**er
but not when the adjective ends in *w*	new	new**er**
For two-syllable adjectives that end in *y*, drop the *y* and add *ier*.	busy	bus**ier**
For most adjectives that have two or more syllables and don't end in *y*, use the word "more."	famous delicious	**more** famous **more** delicious

A Listen and write the adjectives that you hear on the lines on the left. After you listen, circle *1 syllable, 2 syllables ending in Y,* or *2 + syllables (no Y)*. Then, write the comparative forms of the adjectives on the lines on the right.

Comparative Form

1. _old_ (1 syllable) 2 syllables ending in Y   2+ syllables (no Y)   _older_
2. _____1 syllable   2 syllables ending in Y   2+ syllables (no Y)   _____
3. _____1 syllable   2 syllables ending in Y   2+ syllables (no Y)   _____
4. _____1 syllable   2 syllables ending in Y   2+ syllables (no Y)   _____
5. _____1 syllable   2 syllables ending in Y   2+ syllables (no Y)   _____
6. _____1 syllable   2 syllables ending in Y   2+ syllables (no Y)   _____
7. _____1 syllable   2 syllables ending in Y   2+ syllables (no Y)   _____
8. _____1 syllable   2 syllables ending in Y   2+ syllables (no Y)   _____
9. _____1 syllable   2 syllables ending in Y   2+ syllables (no Y)   _____
10. _____1 syllable   2 syllables ending in Y   2+ syllables (no Y)   _____

B These two restaurants, Peter's Fast Food and Pierre's Slow Food, are very different. Complete the sentences below with the comparative form of each adjective in parentheses.

1. Peter's Fast Food is (cheap) .... *cheaper* ....
2. Pierre's Slow Food is (expensive) ....
3. Peter's is (busy) .... and (noisy) ....
4. Pierre's is (old) .... and (famous) ....
5. Pierre's is (large) ....
6. Peter's is (new) ....

C Pierre needs to hire a chef. Compare two people. On the lines below, write sentences using the comparative forms of the adjectives in parentheses. Then decide which chef Pierre should hire. Talk about your decision with a partner.

Daniel	Margaret
30 years of experience	5 years of experience
friendly	very friendly
creative	very creative
very famous	not famous
55 years old	30 years old
impatient	patient

1. ...... *Daniel is more experienced.* .... (experienced)
2. .... (friendly)
3. .... (creative)
4. .... (famous)
5. .... (patient)

I think Pierre should hire .... because ....

....

....

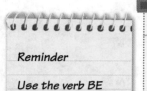

LESSON 61

Comparative Adjectives—Statements and Questions

Reminder

Use the verb BE with adjectives.

You can use a comparative adjective + *than* to compare TWO people, places, or things.

Statements:

My father is **older than** my uncle.
His house is **more modern than** her house.

Hamburgers are **better* than** hot dogs.
My photo is **worse* than** your photo.

Yes-No Questions:

Is your dad **older than** your uncle?

Are they **younger than** you?

Who/Which-Questions:

To compare two people, ask:

Who is ...., [X or Y]?
Who is older, your uncle or your father?
Who is taller?

To compare two places or things, ask:

Which ....is ...., [X or Y]?
Which dessert is healthier?
Which school is better, Kennedy or King?

Which is ...., [X or Y]?
Which is healthier?
Which is better, Kennedy or King?

Language Note:

*The adjectives *good* and *bad* have irregular comparative forms:
              good → **better**   bad → **worse**

A Steve is showing a picture of his big family to his girlfriend, Laura. Read the conversation and fill in the blanks with comparative adjectives. Use your imagination. Then listen to the conversation to hear what comparative adjectives are used.

Laura: Can I see a picture of your family?

Steve: Sure . . . here's one. It's from our family reunion last summer. This is my father and this is my uncle.

Laura: Who's older?

Steve: My father's ...._older_........ . He's sixty-one and my uncle is fifty-eight. And here's my father's sister. She's ....than they are. I think she's fifty-five.

Laura: Do you have any cousins?

Steve: Do I have any cousins? I think I have about thirty! Here's Jeff — he learned to read when he was only two years old. He's really intelligent.

Laura: Is he ....than you?

Steve: Well . . . probably. But I'm ....than he is. And I'm ....

B Write sentences about Steve and Laura with comparative adjectives + *than*. Different sentences are possible.

1. Steve's family is big. Laura's family is small.

   Steve's family is bigger than Laura's family.

   OR Laura's family is smaller than Steve's family.

2. Laura's job is interesting. Steve's job isn't very interesting.

   ....

3. Steve is tall. Laura is medium-height.

   ....

4. Steve's apartment is nice. Laura's apartment isn't very nice.

   ....

5. Laura's roommate is noisy and she never washes the dishes. Steve's roommate is noisy, he never washes the dishes, and he never cleans his room.

   ....

6. Steve's dog is old and lazy. Laura's dog is young and active.

   ....

C Write three questions with this pattern: *Which is (comparative adjective), X or Y?* Then ask three classmates your questions and write their answers in the chart.

EXAMPLE: Q: *Which is better, American food or Chinese food?*
            A: *Chinese food is better.*

Questions:

1. ....

2. ....

3. ....

Name	Answers
	1. 2. 3.
	1. 2. 3.
	1. 2. 3.

Superlative Adjectives—Spelling

Use *the* + a superlative adjective to compare THREE or more people, places, or things.
Peter is **tall**. Pierre is **taller**. Daniela is **the tallest**.

	Adjectives	Superlative Adjectives
For one-syllable adjectives: • add *est*	old	**the oldest**
• add *st* when the adjective ends in *e*	late	**the latest**
• double the final consonant and add *est* when the adjective ends in CVC (consonant + vowel + consonant)	big	**the biggest**
but not when the adjective ends in *w*.	new	**the newest**
For two-syllable adjectives that end in *y*, drop the *y* and add *iest*.	busy	**the busiest**
For most adjectives that have two or more syllables and don't end in *y*, use the words "the most."	famous delicious	**the most** famous **the most** delicious

A Listen and write the adjectives that you hear on the lines on the left. After you listen, circle *1 syllable, 2 syllables ending in Y,* or *2 + syllables (no Y)*. Then, write the superlative forms of the adjectives on the lines on the right.

Superlative Form

1. _old_ (1 syllable) 2 syllables ending in Y   2+ syllables (no Y)   _the oldest_
2. _____1 syllable   2 syllables ending in Y   2+ syllables (no Y)   _____
3. _____1 syllable   2 syllables ending in Y   2+ syllables (no Y)   _____
4. _____1 syllable   2 syllables ending in Y   2+ syllables (no Y)   _____
5. _____1 syllable   2 syllables ending in Y   2+ syllables (no Y)   _____
6. _____1 syllable   2 syllables ending in Y   2+ syllables (no Y)   _____
7. _____1 syllable   2 syllables ending in Y   2+ syllables (no Y)   _____
8. _____1 syllable   2 syllables ending in Y   2+ syllables (no Y)   _____
9. _____1 syllable   2 syllables ending in Y   2+ syllables (no Y)   _____
10. _____1 syllable   2 syllables ending in Y   2+ syllables (no Y)   _____

B Peter and Daniela, are comparing three TVs. Complete each sentence with the number of a TV and the superlative form of the adjective in parentheses. Then decide which TV they should buy. Talk about your decision with a partner.

Electronics

 TV 1
13" screen
$75
38 pounds

 TV 2
20" screen
$225
74 pounds
Built-in VCR

 TV 3
17" flat screen
with DVD/CD
$295
50 pounds

1. TV __1__ is (small) *the smallest* _____.
2. TV _____ is (big) _____.
3. TV _____ is (wide) _____.
4. TV _____ is (expensive) _____.
5. TV _____ is (cheap) _____.
6. TV _____ is (heavy) _____.
7. TV _____ is (light) _____.
8. TV _____ is (modern) _____.

I think Peter and Daniela should buy TV _____ because _____

_____

C Peter and Daniela are also comparing three houses. Write sentences below about the houses. Use the superlative forms of adjectives in parentheses. Then decide which house they should buy. Talk about your decision with a partner.

House 1	House 2	House 3
32 years old	10 years old	67 years old
modern	very modern	old-fashioned
$100,000	$200,000	$150,000
needs paint	looks OK	beautiful
has one bedroom	has two bedrooms	has four bedrooms
not very nice	nice	very nice

1. *House 3 is the oldest* (old)   5. _____ (beautiful)
2. _____ (new)   6. _____ (big)
3. _____ (modern)   7. _____ (small)
4. _____ (nice)   8. _____ (expensive)

I think Peter and Daniela should buy House _____ because _____

_____

LESSON 63

Superlative Adjectives—Statements and Questions

Use *the* + a superlative adjective to compare THREE or more people, places, or things.

Statements:
• I have two sisters and a brother. My brother is **the oldest**, and I'm **the youngest**.
• **The biggest** country in the world is Russia.
• The Sears Tower isn't **the tallest** building in the world.

Yes-No Questions:

Is Russia **the biggest** country in the world?

Who/Which Questions:

To compare three or more people, ask:

Who is ...., [X, Y, or Z]?
Who is the oldest, you, your brother, or your sister?
Who is the youngest?

To compare three or more places or things, ask:

Which is .... , [X, Y, or Z]?	**Which** .... is .... , [X, Y or Z]?
Which is **the best**, San Francisco, Paris, or your hometown?	**Which city** is **the best**, San Francisco, Paris, or your hometown?
Which is **the most** polluted?	**Which city** is **the most** polluted?

Language Note:

The adjectives *good* and *bad* have irregular superlative forms:
good → **the best**   bad → **the worst**

A Underline the superlative adjectives in the following questions. Then listen to the information about places in the world. Circle the correct answers to the questions.

What is . . .

1.	<u>the biggest</u> country in the world?	(Russia)	Canada	the U.S.
2.	the smallest country?	Vatican City	Monaco	Malta
3.	the most populated country?	India	the U.S.	China
4.	the most populated city?	Mexico City	Karachi	Bombay
5.	the biggest ocean in the world?	the Atlantic Ocean	the Pacific Ocean	the Indian Ocean
6.	the longest river?	the Rio Grande	the Amazon	the Nile

194

B Write sentences with the superlative forms of the adjectives in parentheses. Use the past tense in number 2.

1. **Buildings**: The Sears Tower (Chicago) Taipei 101 (Taiwan) The Petronas Towers
   442 meters/1450 feet 508 meters 1667 feet (Kuala Lumpur, Malaysia)
   1974 2004 452 meters/1483 feet
                     1998

(tall) .... building.

(old) .... building.

(new) .... building.

2. **Pollution**   Los Angeles   San Diego   Sacramento
   in California   (number 1)   (number 20)   (number 6)
   cities in 2003:

(polluted).. city in California in 2003.

3. **Bridges**:   The Golden Gate Bridge   The Tsing Ma Bridge   The Brooklyn Bridge
   (San Francisco)   (Hong Kong)   (New York)
   1280 meters/4200 feet   1377 meters/4518 feet 486 meters/1596 feet
   1937   1997   1883

(long) .... bridge.

(short) .... bridge.

(old) .... bridge.

C Write three questions with this pattern: *"Which (or Who) is (superlative adjective), X, Y or Z?"* Then ask two classmates your questions and write their answers in the chart.

EXAMPLE: Q: *Which is the best place to live, Tokyo, Paris, or your hometown?*
          A: *My town is the best.*

Questions:

1. ....

2. ....

3. ....

Name	Answers
	1. 2. 3.
	1. 2. 3.

Contrast: Comparative and Superlative Adjectives

Use comparative adjectives to compare TWO people, places, or things. Use superlative adjectives to compare THREE or more people, places, or things.

	Adjectives	Comparative Adjectives	Superlative Adjectives
One-syllable adjectives:	fast large big	faster (than) larger (than) bigger (than)	the fastest the largest the biggest
Two-syllable adjectives that end in y:	funny	funnier (than)	the funniest
Adjectives that have two or more syllables and don't end in y:	beautiful	more beautiful (than)	the most beautiful
Irregular forms:	good bad	better (than) worse (than)	the best the worst

A A TV announcer is talking about some of the athletes at the Winter Olympics. Read the following paragraphs and circle the correct words from those in parentheses. Then listen and check your answers.

That's Chris Leon from the Canadian team. He's (1. faster/ the fastest) skier from Canada. He can ski (2. faster than/the fastest) his father, who was an Olympic champion many years ago.

Mark Brewer is a speed skater. He's (3. older/the oldest) skater on his team, but he's (4. the strongest/stronger) and (5. faster/the fastest). I met Mark a few years ago and really enjoyed talking to him. He's (6. funnier/the funniest), (7. friendlier/the friendliest) and (8. more interesting/the most interesting) athlete I know. Maybe that's why he's (9. the most popular/more popular) athlete in Canada. He's (10. the most popular/more popular than) movie stars!

B Write sentences about these Summer Olympic athletes. Use comparative and superlative adjectives. More than one answer may be possible.

1. Connie is a fast swimmer. Sherry is a very fast swimmer.

   Sherry is faster than Connie. OR Connie is slower than Sherry.

2. Connie is a good swimmer. Sherry is a very good swimmer.

   _____

3. Amy is a pretty good swimmer. Connie is a good swimmer. Sherry is a very good swimmer.

   _____

4. My brother is a bad swimmer. And I'm a terrible swimmer.

   _____

5. My sister and brother are bad swimmers. I'm a terrible swimmer.

   _____ *in my family.*

6. Tony isn't a popular gymnast. Roger is a popular gymnast.

   _____

7. Tony isn't a popular gymnast. Roger is a popular gymnast. Rick is a very popular gymnast.

   _____

 C Chant

Interesting Job

His job is much more interesting than hers,
But it's more difficult and much more dangerous.
Her office is bigger. Her salary is higher
But his job is much more interesting than hers.

    What's his job?
    What does he do?
He's a lion tamer.
He works at the zoo.

My job's the best. It's better than the rest.
I work at the zoo, too.
I dust teddy bears in the gift shop
Every day from ten to two.

Review

Comparative and Superlative Adjectives

A **Dictation** Two students are talking about learning English. Listen and write what you hear. Key words: *grammar, spelling*

1.
Student 1: *What's harder for you?*
Student 2: ....

2.
Student 1: ....
Student 2: ....
....

3.
Student 1: ....
Student 2: ....
....

B Complete this chart with comparative and superlative adjectives.

Adjectives	Comparative Adjectives	Superlative Adjectives
young	younger	the youngest
	funnier	
hot		
crowded		
		the healthiest
easy		
exciting		
	better	
bad		

198

C Look at the following groups of words. Write sentences with the comparative forms of the adjectives in parentheses. Give your opinion.

EXAMPLE:

TV programs/movies (good) _I think movies are better than TV programs._

1. chocolate ice cream/strawberry ice cream (delicious)

   ....

2. salad/candy (healthy)

   ....

3. cold weather/hot weather (bad)

   ....

4. rock music/classical music (good)

   ....

5. learning a foreign language/learning to drive (easy)

   ....

6. going to a party/going to the movies (enjoyable)

   ....

D Ask a partner the following questions. Take notes. Then, on a separate piece of paper, write six sentences about your partner.

EXAMPLE: Adriana thinks it's better to sit in the front of the classroom because she can see the board and hear the teacher.

1. Do you think it is better to sit in the front or the back of the classroom? Why?

2. Which is the hardest for you—reading, writing, speaking, or understanding English? Why?

3. Which is the easiest for you—reading, writing, speaking, or understanding English? Why?

4. Which is the best for you—working alone, working with a partner, or working with a group? Why?

5. What do you think is the fastest way to learn a language?

6. What activity in our class is the most fun? Why?

Have Fun

A Crossword Puzzle

The crossword puzzle grid, with 8 across filled in as "interesting".

Across

1. They have three sizes of popcorn at the movies and we chose the ....
5. She works and has six kids. She's the .... person I know.
7. My dog never does anything. He's .... than your dog.
8. This book is OK, but that book is more ....
10. We went to the most .... beach last summer.
11. I'm the baby in the family. I'm the ....
12. We went to three bad movies. Two were very bad, and the last one was the ....

Down

2. They looked at three cars and bought the most .... one.
3. Your cat is smart. It's the most .... cat I know.
4. English is .... than my native language.
6. Your neighborhood is noisy, but my neighborhood is ....
9. It was the .... movie I ever saw and I cried and cried.
10. My father is the .... cook in the family. Everything he makes is delicious.

B Chart

Progress Report

Everybody says I sound better this year.
My accent is better than it was last year.
My grammar is better, much better.
My English is better than it was last year.

Writing is easier than it was last year.
My spelling is better, my sentences are longer.
My grammar is stronger than it was last year.
The homework is easier and much more interesting.

Our classroom is larger and much more comfortable.
The desks are bigger, the seats are wider.
Everything is better than it was last year.

I'm not the worst student and I'm not the best
But my mother tells me I'm better than the rest.

Appendices

Appendix A

60 Irregular Verbs

Base Form	Past Form	Base Form	Past Form
be	was/were	lose (one O)	lost
begin	began	make	made
break	broke	meet	met
bring	brought	pay	paid
buy	bought	put	put
catch	caught	read	read (pronounce *red*)
choose	chose	ride	rode
come	came	ring	rang
cost	cost	run	ran
cut	cut	say	said (rhymes with *bed*)
do	did	see	saw
drink	drank	sell	sold
drive	drove	send	sent
eat	ate (like 8)	sing	sang
fall	fell (2 Ls)	sit	sat
feel	felt (1 L)	sleep	slept
find	found	speak	spoke
fly	flew	spend	spent
forget	forgot	stand	stood
get	got	swim	swam
give	gave	take	took
go	went	teach	taught
grew	grow	tell	told
have	had	think	thought
hear	heard (rhymes with *word*)	throw	threw
hold	held	understand	understood
hurt	hurt	wake up	woke up
keep	kept	wear	wore
know	knew (silent "k")	win	won
leave	left	write	wrote

Appendix B

Irregular Verb Memorization Groups

[P=Pronunciation Difference]

No change:	ought:	ew:	got:	ang:
cost - cost	bring - brought	blow - blew	get - got	ring - rang
cut- cut	buy - bought	draw - drew	forget - forgot	sing - sang
fit - fit	fight - fought	fly - flew		
hit - hit	think - thought	grow - grew		
hurt - hurt	BUT:	know - knew		
let - let	catch - caught	throw - threw		
put - put	teach - taught			
quit - quit				
read - read (P)				
set - set				
oke:	**aid:**	**ent:**	**stood:**	**old:**
speak - spoke	say - said	send - sent	stand - stood	sell - sold
break - broke	pay - paid (P)	spend - spent	understand - understood	tell - told
wake - woke				

Appendix C

Comparison of Question Forms with BE

Present, Past, and Future (with *BE going to*)

	Statement	Yes-No Question	Wh-Question
I	I am happy. I was happy. I am going to be happy.	Am I happy? Was I happy? Am I going to be happy?	When am I happy? When was I happy? When am I going to be happy?
She/He/It	He is a teacher. He was a teacher. He is going to be a teacher.	Is he a teacher? Was he a teacher? Is he going to be a teacher?	Why is he a teacher? Why was he a teacher? Why is he going to be a teacher?
You/We/They	They are in the store. They were in the store. They are going to be in the store.	Are they in the store? Were they in the store? Are they going to be in the store?	Where are they? Where were they? Where are they going to be?

* Use *be* with adjectives, nouns, and places.

Appendix D

Verb Tense Charts

1. Comparison of present, past, and future (with will) tenses

Verb Tense	Affirmative	Negative	Yes-No Question	Wh-Question
Present I, You, We, They	They work here.	They **don't** (**do** not) work here.	**Do** they work here?	Where **do** they work?
Present He, She, It	He work**s** here.	He **doesn't** (**does** not) work here.	**Does** he work here?	Where **does** he work?
Past I, You, He, She, It, We, They	She work**ed** here.	She **didn't** (**did** not) work here.	**Did** she work here?	Where **did** she work?
Future with *will* I, You, He, She, It, We, They	We'll (we **will**) work here.	We **won't** (**will** not) work here.	**Will** we work here?	Where **will** we work?

2. Present Continuous Tense

	Affirmative	Negative	Yes-No Question	WH-Question
I	I'**m** work**ing** here.	I'**m** not work**ing** here.	**Am** I work**ing** here?	Where **am** I work**ing**?
You, We, They	We'**re** work**ing** here.	We **aren't** work**ing** here.	**Are** we work**ing** here?	Where **are** we work**ing**?
He, She, It	She'**s** work**ing** here.	She **isn't** work**ing** here.	**Is** she work**ing** here?	Where **is** she work**ing**?

3. Future with *be going to*

	Affirmative	Negative	Yes-No Question	WH-Question
I	I'**m** go**ing** to work here.	I'**m** not go**ing** to work here.	**Am** I go**ing** to work here?	Where **am** I go**ing** to work?
You, We, They	You'**re** go**ing** to work here.	You'**re** not go**ing** to work here.	**Are** you go**ing** to work here?	Where **are** you go**ing** to work?
He, She, It	He'**s** go**ing** to work here.	He'**s** not go**ing** to work here.	**Is** he go**ing** to work here?	Where **is** he go**ing** to work?

Appendix E

Time Expressions

Present Tense	Present Continuous Tense	Past Tense	Future Tense
every	now	*yesterday*	today
second	right now	morning	tomorrow
minute	at this moment	afternoon	the day after
hour		evening	tomorrow
day	these days		
month		the day before yesterday	*in*
year	**Present Continuous Tense**		an hour
morning	**to show Future Meaning**	*last*	two weeks
afternoon		night	2050
evening	today	week	
night	tomorrow	month	*next*
spring	at noon	year	week
summer	at 6:00	spring	month
winter	next week	summer	year
fall	next month	fall	
		winter	*at*
on	*in*		noon
Sunday**s**	a few minutes	*in*	midnight
Monday**s**	five minutes	1950	6:00
weekday**s**	an hour	the 20th century	
weekend**s**			*on*
	this	*at*	Sunday
once a week	morning	noon	Monday
twice a week	afternoon	midnight	
three times a month	evening	6:00	*this*
	week		morning
Frequency Adverbs:	weekend	*Ago:*	afternoon
always	month	an hour ago	evening
usually	year	a year ago	week
often	Saturday	two years ago	weekend
sometimes			month
rarely		*When*	year
hardly ever		I was 16	Saturday
never		you arrived	
		she was in school	

Appendix F

Modals

Modals	Affirmative	Negative	Yes-No Questions
will	I will see you tomorrow.	I won't see you tomorrow.	Will I see you tomorrow?
can	She can help us.	She can't help us.	Can she help us?
could	When he was ten, he could run very fast.	When he was ten, he couldn't vote.	Could he run very fast when he was ten?
should	You should come to class early.	You shouldn't come to class late.	Should we come to class early?

Appendix G

Special Nouns

Irregular Nouns

Singular	Plural (these words do not end in s)
a man, one man	men
a woman, one woman	women
a person, one person	people
a child, one child	children
a foot, one foot	feet
a tooth, one tooth	teeth

Nouns that are always plural—*Don't use a/an with these nouns.*

glasses*
pants*
jeans*
shorts*
clothes
groceries

*These are each one thing, with two connected parts.

Appendix H

Common Non-Count Nouns

Food:	Liquids:
bread	beer
butter	coffee
candy	cream
cheese	juice
fruit	milk
gum	soda
lettuce	soup
meat	tea
sugar	water
toast	wine

Other non-count nouns and their related count nouns

furniture	a table, a chair, a sofa, a desk
garbage	
homework	an assignment
information	a fact, an opinion
jewelry	a necklace, a bracelet
knowledge	a fact, an opinion
luggage	a suitcase
mail	a letter, a postcard
make-up	
money	a dollar, a quarter, a dime, a nickel, a penny
music	a song, a symphony
noise	
paper	a newspaper
pollution	
scenery	a view
slang	a word, an expression, an idiom
software	a computer program
traffic	
time	an hour, a minute, a second
vocabulary	a word, an expression, an idiom

Appendix I

Prepositions of Time and Place

TIME

in	on	at	from...to...
A month: in April **A year:** in 2004 **A season:** in the summer **Parts of a day:** in the morning in the afternoon in the evening **The future:** in ten minutes in a half hour in two years	**A day:** on Monday on my birthday on New Year's Day on Saturday morning on Sunday night **A date:** on January 1st on the 4th of July on March 28th, 1978	**A time:** at 3:00 p.m. at 1 o'clock at noon at midnight **Part of a day:** at night	**from ___ to ___:** from 9:00 to 11:00 from Saturday to Sunday from 2005 to 2006

PLACE

in	on	at	from....to...
A city: in New York **A state:** in Florida **A country:** in Canada **A room:** in the kitchen **A location:** in the front of in the back of	**A street:** on Fifth Avenue **On public transportation:** on a bus on a plane on a train on a boat	**An address:** at 1600 Fifth Avenue **Places:** at home at work at school	**from ___ to ___:** from Los Angeles to Mexico City

Appendix J

Phrases with Prepositions

Common Verb and Preposition Combinations

arrive **in** the city
arrive **in** Canada
arrive **at** the airport
ask someone **about** a schedule
ask someone **for** help
come **from** China
come **to** school
go **to** work
live **in** a house
listen **to** music
look **at** a painting
look **for** my keys
pay attention **to** the teacher
register **for** a class
shop **for** groceries
talk **about** my vacation
talk **to** my friend
stay **at** a hotel
walk **to** school
take care **of** my baby
thank you **for** the gift
welcome **to** the U.S.

Common Adjective and Preposition Combinations

be...
absent **from** class
afraid **of** dogs
excited **about** my trip
famous **for** good food
full **of** smoke
good **at** sports
interested **in** soccer
late **for** work
worried **about** my future
proud **of** my son
tired **of** my job
worried **about** my homework

Communication Gap Instructions for Student A

Have Fun Lessons 56–59, page 186

Exercise A

STUDENT A: Read these directions to Student B so he or she can draw the picture below. Do not let Student B see this page.

1. Draw a rectangular school with three floors in the middle of the box.
2. Put a door in the middle of the first floor.
3. Give the school six windows on each floor.
4. Write "School of the Arts" over the door.
5. Put flowers in front of the building.
6. Draw a sunny sky with some birds flying.
7. Put a big tree on the right.
8. Draw two people under the tree. They are talking to each other.

Communication Gap Instructions for Student B

Have Fun Lessons 56–59, page 186

Exercise A

STUDENT B: Read these directions to Student A so he or she can draw the picture below. Do not let Student A see this page.

1. Draw a house. Put it in the middle of the box.
2. Put a front door in the middle of the house.
3. Put a window on the left and on the right side of the door.
4. Put a chimney on the top right side of the house.
5. Have smoke come out of the chimney.
6. On the right, put a tree next to the house.
7. Put a dog under the tree.
8. Draw clouds in the sky.
9. Write your name in the bottom right corner of the box.

Listening Script

Lesson 1

A

1. people, class
2. room
3. students, teacher
4. sweater, pants
5. things, desk, plant, books, apple
6. men, VCR
7. students, notebooks

Lesson 2

A

new, small, comfortable, beautiful, quiet, safe, lucky, friendly, homesick, delicious, cold, warm, expensive, favorite

Lesson 3

A

Jose's alarm clock rings every day at 5:00 a.m. He gets up and eats breakfast. Then he takes the bus to work.

He works all day. After work, he plays soccer with his friends. At night, he is very tired. He watches TV and then goes to bed. He is far away from his family. He misses his family very much.

Lesson 4

A

Good afternoon, everyone. My name is Mark. Welcome to Milton College. Our tour begins today at the campus bookstore. You can buy books, school supplies, and even toothpaste at the store. We'll come back here at the end of the tour.

First, we'll walk to the art building. You'll see some examples of student art on the second floor. Then we'll go to the administra-tion building. This is a busy time for us. The fall semester begins on Wednesday, so right now many students are registering for their classes. Our students come from all over the world. I'll give you a chance to talk to them after the tour.

Lesson 5

A

MC: Welcome to our show. Today we are talking to people who have unusual jobs. Excuse me, sir.
Bart: Yes.
MC: Welcome to our program, "Unusual Jobs." What's your name?
Bart: My name is Bart Highsmith.
MC: And what is your unusual job?
Bart: I work on bridges. I paint bridges.
MC: Wow. That sounds dangerous!
Bart: It is dangerous, but I like high places. And I make a lot of money.
MC: That's wonderful! Thank you, Bart. Uh, Sir. Could you tell me your name?
Mel: My name is Mel.
MC: Hi, Mel. And what is your unusual job?
Mel: I shop.
MC: You shop?
Mel: Yes. Some people don't have time to shop. So I shop for them.
MC: What a terrific job!
Mel: It's a great job. I love it!
MC: And you two. What are your names and what are your jobs?
Mark: I'm Mark Magnum. I train lions for the circus.
MC: Wow!
Fran: I'm Fran Fido, and I walk dogs.
MC: How many dogs can you walk at one time?
Fran: Oh, about 5 or 6. I can make a lot of money walking dogs.
MC: Well thank you, Fran and Mark. That's all for today. See you next week when we'll bring you unusual hobbies.

Review: Lessons 1–5

A

My name is Lisa. This is my family. I have three children. My sons are six and eight. My daughter is two years old. My husband is a good cook. My father is a good cook, too. But he's tired today.

Lesson 6

A

Mark: Mmm. This food is delicious.
Julie: Thank you! We have many good cooks in this neighborhood.
Mark: You're lucky! Uh…My name is Mark.
Julie: Hi, Mark. I'm Julie.
Mark: Nice to meet you, Julie. It's a beautiful day for a party.
Julie: It sure is. Are you a new neighbor?
Mark: No. My mother-in-law Kathy lives here. My wife and I are here for her birthday.
Julie: Oh! You're Kathy's son-in-law! You're from Hong Kong.
Mark: That's right.
Julie: Do you like Hong Kong?
Mark: Yes, but life in Hong Kong is very expensive. And the traffic is terrible.
Julie: Kathy said you work in a hospital.
Mark: That's right, but I'm not a doctor. I'm a computer programmer.
Julie: Is your family with you?
Mark: My wife is here, but my children aren't with us. They're

visiting their grandparents.
Julie: How old are your children?
Mark: Well, my daughter is 10 years old and my son is 15.
Julie: My son is 15, too! Well, enjoy the party. It was nice to meet you.
Mark: Nice to meet you, too!

Lesson 7

A

Mom: Hi, Jake.
Jake: Hi, Mom.
Mom: Are you tired? Are you in bed?
Jake: Mom! It's 5:00 a.m. here in California!
Mom: Oh, I'm sorry. How are all of you? Are the kids OK?
Jake: We're all fine, Mom!
Mom: How is the weather? Is it cold out?
Jake: No, it's very nice.
Mom: And how is the hotel? Are the beds comfortable? Is the food good?
Jake: Everything is wonderful.
Mom: How about the rooms? Are the rooms noisy?
Jake: No, they're not. They're fine. Can I talk to you later, Mom?
Mom: Oh, I'm sorry. You're tired. But one more question. Is the hotel expensive?
Jake: Well, it's a little expensive, but it's really nice.

Lesson 8

A

Host: Well, it's time to play The Marriage Game! Are you ready, Tom?
Husband: Yes, I am.
Host: OK. For 10 points, question number one: When is Laura's birthday?
Husband: That's easy. September 20.
Host: You're right. That's 10 points. Question number two, what is her favorite color?
Husband: Uh…Green?

Host: You're wrong. Her favorite color is red! Sorry. Next question. Where is your wife from?
Husband: That's easy, too. New York.
Host: Correct! And number 4, what nationality are her parents?
Husband: That's easy. …Brazilian!
Host: That's 10 points. Now, I'm sure you know this one. Number 5. What color are your wife's eyes?
Husband: Uh…blue…no green….no, blue.
Host: I'm sorry. Your wife wrote "green."
Wife: Look at my eyes! They're green!
Host: OK. Question number 6. Who is your wife's best friend?
Husband: I am, of course.
Host: I'm sorry. Your wife wrote "Tina."
Wife: Oops!
Host: Now, your last question. When is your wedding anniversary?
Husband: Wait! I know…I know… It's …today!
Host: You're right! Congratulations!
Wife: I love you, honey!
Host: I'm sorry. You didn't win the car. But thanks for playing The Marriage Game!

Review: Lessons 6–8

A

Bob: Hi, are you a student here?
Marie: No, I'm not. I'm on vacation. I'm here with my parents.
Bob: Where are you from?
Marie: I'm from Peru.
Bob: Wow! Peru is far from here! Well, you're lucky. The weather is beautiful this week.
Marie: You're right! It's not very cold. We're lucky.

Lesson 10

A

Dan: Hi, Linda! I found an apartment!
Linda: That's great! Where is it?
Dan: It's near the campus. I like it, but there aren't any supermarkets in the neighborhood.
Linda: That's too bad. How much is the apartment?
Dan: It's a little expensive. It's $900 a month.
Linda: How big is it?
Dan: It's pretty big! There are two bedrooms, but there's only one bathroom.
Linda: That's OK. You only need one bathroom. Is there a bath tub?
Dan: No, there's just a shower.
Linda: Is there a dining room?
Dan: No there isn't, but there's a big table in the kitchen.
Linda: How about a dishwasher? Is there a dishwasher?
Dan: Yeah. And there's a laundry room in the basement.
Linda: How about parking? Is there a garage?
Dan: There isn't a garage, but there's a parking lot near the building.
Linda: What floor is the apartment on?
Dan: It's on the 6th floor.
Linda: The 6th floor! Is there an elevator?
Dan: No, there isn't. It's an old building.
Linda: That's terrible.
Dan: It's OK. I need the exercise.

Lesson 11

A

1. My name is Juan, and I'm a waiter at the Calypso Restaurant.
2. I'm from Uruguay. It's a very small country in South America.
3. It's south of Brazil.

4. Its capital is Montevideo.
5. This is a picture of my brother. His name is David.
6. He's thirty years old, and he's married.
7. He and his wife both work in the U.S.
8. They're both accountants. Their jobs are very difficult.
9. They have a son and a daughter. Their daughter is a doctor. Her name is Lucia.
10. Their son is a university student. He's twenty-one years old.
11. We're in the U.S., but our parents are still in Uruguay.

Review: Lessons 9–11

A

A: Excuse me. Is there a pharmacy near here?
B: I think there's a pharmacy on Center Street.
A: Center Street? How far is it from here?
B: It's not far. It's around the corner.

Lesson 12

A

Javier and his uncle Ernesto live in the same apartment. They both come from Mexico. They work in the same expensive restaurant. But they don't see each other very much. Why not?

They have different work schedules. Javier works during the evening, but Ernesto doesn't work during the evening. He goes to work early in the morning and goes to sleep early.

Ernesto has the "graveyard shift." He wakes up at 3:00 a.m., leaves the house at 3:30, and works from 4:00 a.m. to noon. Then he comes home, has lunch, and goes to bed at 7:00 p.m.

Javier is a waiter at the restaurant. He begins work at 5:00 p.m.

He doesn't go to bed until late at night. He stays in bed until almost noon. He takes the bus to work at 4:30 p.m. When he comes home, his uncle Ernesto is in bed.

Javier and Ernesto don't work on Sundays and Mondays. They don't do anything on those days. They just stay home and relax.

Lesson 13

A

1. What does Javier do?
2. Where does Javier work?
3. Does he work every day?
4. Does he get tips?
5. Do the waiters wear uniforms?
6. How many days a week does he work?
7. Why does he like his job?

Lesson 14

A

Mark: How's your son Sam?
Julia: Oh, he's fine, but he's very lazy. He hardly ever does his homework! He goes to bed so late that he's usually tired in the morning. Of course, he's always late for school. And he hardly ever gets As on his report card!
Mark: Does he ever help you around the house?
Julia: He never does! When he has free time, he almost always plays on the computer. When he takes off his clothes, he usually leaves them on the floor. He hardly ever picks them up. I don't know what to do.
Mark: Do you ever punish him?
Julia: Hardly ever.
Mark: Hmm. Maybe that's the problem!

Review 12–15

A

I have an exciting life. I'm hardly ever bored. During the week, I leave the house at 7:00

a.m. and go to work. Then I stop for dinner and do some homework. On Mondays and Wednesdays, I study English. On the weekends, I like to go dancing. I don't go to bed until 2:00 a.m. I enjoy my life.

Lesson 16

A

My name is Sara. I have two children, Paula and Henry. They're both in high school. They speak perfect English.

Paula is the oldest. She's very good at sports, but she isn't a very good student. She doesn't like to do her homework. She plays soccer for her school. Her room is full of trophies. Paula wants to be in the Olympics some day. She doesn't want to go to college.

Henry isn't athletic. He doesn't like to play any sports. But he loves music. He practices the piano five hours a day, so he doesn't have much time for schoolwork. He plays classical music and jazz. He's very talented.

Lesson 17

A

1. Are you usually happy?
2. Do you go to many parties?
3. Do you enjoy quiet places?
4. Do you read a lot every day?
5. Are you often on the phone?
6. Are you often late for school?
7. Do you eat at restaurants alone?
8. Do you like to be alone?

Lesson 18

A

1. Where is San Francisco?
2. What does the name San Francisco mean?
3. What is San Francisco famous for?

4. How much do hotels cost in San Francisco?
5. What do people love to do in San Francisco?
6. How is the weather in San Francisco?
7. Why do many tourists come to San Francisco?

Lesson 19

A

1. My name is Heather. My parents and I live in this house. We like the neighborhood, but we have problems with some of our neighbors.
2. This is Mr. Parker. He lives next door to us. He plays the trumpet every morning at 6:00 a.m. We like him, but we don't like his trumpet.
3. This is Morgan and his wife Susie. They live next door to Mr. Parker. We have problems with them because they have a very unfriendly dog. Their dog barks every night.
4. This is Mrs. Rivera. She lives across the street from us. She is 80 years old. We like her because she bakes chocolate chip cookies for us every Sunday. Her cookies are delicious!

Review: Lessons 16–19

A

My son is very lucky. He has a beautiful family, makes a lot of money, and is healthy. His wife loves him very much. His children are excellent students. Their teachers always give them As.

Lesson 20

A

1. A: Hello. Is Mr. Jones there?
   B: Yes, but he's talking to a client right now. Can I take a message?

2. A: Hi. Where are you?
   B: I'm having coffee in a café on Market Street. Where are you?
   A: I'm walking down Market Street. What's the name of the café?
   B: I don't know, but a band is playing in front of the cafe.
   A: Oh. OK. I see it. I'm crossing the street right now.
3. A: I can meet you on the corner in fifteen minutes. It's raining. Don't forget your umbrella.
   B: It's not raining here! The sun is shining.
   A: Really? That's strange!
4. A: Please leave a message after the beep.
   B: Mom! Mom! Where are you? We're waiting for you at school! Hello. Oh, no. She's not home!

Lesson 21

A

Susan: Hi. Mom! How are you?
Mom: Fine. How are you doing?
Susan: We're doing fine.
Mom: Are you having a good time?
Susan: Yes, we are. We're having a wonderful time.
Mom: What are you doing now?
Susan: Well, I'm sitting in the sun. I'm enjoying the beautiful weather. What are you doing?
Mom: I'm not sitting in the sun! It's raining here in Boston. I'm paying my bills. What is Bob doing?
Susan: He's cooking dinner.
Mom: Really? What's he cooking?
Susan: Well, he's not really cooking. He's barbecuing some hamburgers.
Mom: Oh….Is the baby sleeping?
Susan: I hope so. Oh… she's crying now. I have to go.
Mom: Wait… when are you coming home?
Susan: Next Monday.
Mom: OK. See you then! Bye.

Lesson 23

A

Stuart: Ida! It smells terrible in here!
What are you doing?
Ida: I'm painting the walls.
Stuart: Why are you painting the walls?
Ida: Because they look terrible!
Stuart: But why are you using pink? I don't like pink.
Ida: But I love pink. Can you help me? I need more paint.
Stuart: OK. But I want to change the color. How about gray?
Ida: Gray! I hate gray. Listen. The phone is ringing. Will you get it?
Stuart: OK.

Review: Lessons 20–23

A

Mark: So, what do you do in your spare time?
Maggie: I don't have a lot of free time. When I'm free, I like to travel.
Mark: Are you going to Toronto for fun?
Maggie: Yes and no. I'm going there for a meeting, but then I'm planning to visit my cousin.

Lesson 24

A

Rob: Look at these things for sale! Here's an ad for a used truck. I need a truck.
Mimi: How old is it?
Rob: It's only 10 years old. It says it has a new engine and new brakes. And it's only $2,000. That's a good price. Let's write down the phone number.
Mimi: Oh, look at this ad! There's a garage sale on Saturday near our new apartment.
Rob: You're right. And they're selling bicycles. We should stop by!
Mimi: And we need a rug. Oh,

here's an ad for a free puppy!
Let's get a puppy!
Rob: But puppies are a lot of work. I don't think we can have puppies in our apartment.
Mimi: I guess you're right. We have a lot of other things to buy first! Let's definitely go to the garage sale. It sounds great.

Lesson 26

A

Lily: Are you ready for the party?
Mike: No, I'm not. How much time do we have before the party?
Lily: We don't have much time. Class begins in fifteen minutes.
Mike: Oh, no! Let's see. I can make the coffee. How much coffee is there?
Lily: I see a whole bag of coffee. There's a lot of coffee.
Mike: Oh, good. Now, how about cups? How many paper cups are there?
Lily: There aren't many cups. How many cups do we need?
Mike: Well, how many students are in our class?
Lily: Thirty. Let's see… there are five cups. We need a lot of cups.
Mike: How much tea is there?
Lily: There isn't any tea.

Lesson 27

A

Good morning, everyone! Today I'm going to show you how to make soy sauce beef.
1. First, you need to get a big bowl.
2. Then, get some soy sauce. You need about three tablespoons.
3. Then put the soy sauce in the bowl.
4. Now peel some garlic and an onion.
5. Chop up the garlic and the onion and put them in the bowl with the soy sauce.
6. Now get some meat. Cut the meat into small pieces and put in the bowl.
7. Then get a frying pan and put some oil in it.
8. Turn on the stove. When the oil is hot, put the meat in the frying pan. Then fry the meat for just a few minutes and your soy sauce beef is ready!

Review Lessons 24–27

A

Clerk: Can I help you?
Danny: Yes, my class is having a party, and I need to buy some cookies.
Clerk: Well, how many people are there in your class?
Danny: I think there are about 30.

Lesson 28

A

Lena: Do you remember our trip here? It was exactly 10 years ago!
Teresa: I remember a little, but I was only 10 years old.
Lena: You weren't 10! I think you were about 12 years old!
Teresa: No. I wasn't 12, Grandma. I was born in 1985.
Lena: OK. OK.
Teresa: I remember that it was a very long trip. But it was exciting.
Lena: Well, it wasn't exciting for me. It was a very long trip. We were on the bus for twenty hours. The weather was bad. And I was so worried about our future
Teresa: But are you happy that we're here now?
Lena: Of course I am.

Lesson 29

A

Leo: What was the homework on Friday?
Cindy: I don't know. I was absent. Were you absent, too?
Leo: Yes, I was really sick. I had a bad cold. We were all sick.
Cindy: Were your children sick, too?
Leo: Yes. Even my cat was sick! So why were you absent?
Cindy: My parents were in town.
Leo: Why were they here?
Cindy: They were here because my sister had a baby. I have a niece!
Leo: Congratulations! When was she born?
Cindy: Last week. We went out to dinner to celebrate.
Leo: Where did you go?
Cindy: We went to Jo's Restaurant.
Leo: Is that the restaurant on College Avenue?
Cindy: It *was* on College Avenue. Now it's on Green Street.
Leo: How was the restaurant? Was the food good?
Cindy: Yes, it was. It was delicious, but the service was a little slow. Hmmm. What time is it? I don't see any other students.
Leo: Oh, that's right! It's a holiday. I forgot!

Lesson 30

A

Ken: Tell me about your hometown.
David: Well, it was a very small town. It was very beautiful. There were a lot of mountains and there was a lake near the town. It was very clean. There was no traffic and no pollution.
Ken: How many people were there in the town?
David: Oh, maybe a hundred people.
Ken: It sounds wonderful.
David: It was beautiful, but there were a lot of problems.
Ken: What were the problems?
David: Well, there weren't many jobs. There were a lot of small farms, but there weren't any factories.
Ken: Were there any stores?
David: Yes, but there weren't

many stores. But there was always fresh milk from the farm. And every Friday night, there was music in the town square.

Review: Lessons 28–30

A

Last night, someone in the kitchen at Hotel Majestic put poison in the mashed potatoes. Some hotel guests were sick, but today they are better. Mrs. Mary Smith was sick, but her husband wasn't. She said, "All of the food was delicious. And the mashed potatoes were wonderful. My husband is on a diet so he didn't eat the potatoes. He was lucky."

Lesson 32

A

Jerry is a student at Holden College. He is very busy because he works all day and studies at night. He doesn't have much free time.

Jerry is usually a good student. He usually does his work, but last night he didn't feel well. He had a cold. He knew he had to study for a test, but he was too tired. And he didn't do his homework. He went to bed early, but this morning, he still felt bad. So he didn't go to school and didn't take the test. He stayed home and watched TV.

Lesson 33

A

Dear Advice Column:
Every Saturday I do the same thing. I clean the house or wash clothes. It's a little boring. Last weekend I wanted to do something different. I decided to get a tattoo. I looked up tattoo shops in the phone book and found one near my house.

I drove to the tattoo shop and went inside. I thought about what I wanted. Finally, I chose a tattoo—a half moon on my arm.

It hurt a little bit, but it wasn't expensive. It cost $25.00.

I came home and showed my tattoo to my children. They said that they loved the tattoo. Now I have a problem. They want tattoos too!

What should I do?
Thanks, Fabiola

Lesson 34

A

I was born in 1975 in a small town in Mexico. I left school when I was 16 years old and got my first job. I worked in a brick factory. It was very hard work. I worked twelve hours every day, six days a week. I only made $2.00 an hour.

About fifteen years ago, I decided to come to the U.S. because I wanted to get a better job. But first, I had to get a visa. I went to Mexico City and stood in line for twelve hours to get it.

Fourteen years ago I took a bus to Los Angeles. On the bus I met a very beautiful woman named Sara. We got married twelve years ago. I studied English for six years after I came to the U.S. Now I'm a manager in a construction company and I have three wonderful children.

Review: Lessons 31–34

A

Annie: Brad! What's wrong? You look upset.
Brad: I am. I missed my grammar test this morning.
Annie: Why? What happened?
Brad: I forgot to change my clock last night before I went to bed. I got up at 8:00, but it was really 9:00! And when I got to school at 10:00, the test was over!
Annie: What did your teacher say?

Brad: She looked surprised when she saw me. When I told her that I didn't change my clock, she laughed. She said the same thing once happened to her.

Lesson 35

A

Last night, my wife and I went to the Island Café for dinner. It's a new restaurant. It opened three weeks ago.

We didn't have a good time. It wasn't a good restaurant, and it wasn't in a nice area. It was very crowded, and we waited for a table for forty-five minutes.

Our table wasn't clean, and the flowers weren't fresh.

Our waiter wasn't polite. He wasn't a good waiter. I ordered salmon, but he didn't bring me salmon. He brought me chicken. My wife ordered spaghetti, but he didn't serve her spaghetti. He served her a hamburger. We weren't happy.

We waited about half an hour, and he finally brought us the right food. We were very hungry, but the food wasn't hot and it didn't taste good. We didn't eat it—we paid and left.

My wife and I didn't like the Island Café. But we were happy after we had some pizza and took a walk on the beach.

Lesson 36

A

Rose: How was brunch yesterday?
Andrew: It was great. We had a really nice time.
Rose: Where did you go?
Andrew: To a restaurant in my neighborhood. They serve breakfast all day.
Rose: Was your mother happy?
Andrew: Yes, very. I gave her a beautiful necklace.
Rose: Was she surprised?
Andrew: She sure was! She cried!

Rose: That's so nice. She's lucky to have you as a son...Is she retired?
Andrew: Uh-huh. She was a teacher for thirty years.
Rose: When did she retire?
Andrew: Uh-I think about two years ago.
Rose: What does she do now?
Andrew: She loves her free time, but twice a week she volunteers at an elementary school.

Lesson 37

A

Two months ago, I fell down the stairs and broke my left leg. I was in a hurry because I was late. When I fell, I made a lot of noise and I felt a lot of pain. It was terrible. I didn't cry, but I wanted to. Luckily, my mom and my brother were home. They ran to help me. My mother sat down and talked to me, and my brother called an ambulance.

Now, I'm standing in front of my high school. I'm much better. I have a cast and I walk with crutches. My leg doesn't hurt, but it isn't easy to walk. I go to school and I go to work. My mom doesn't want me to work, but I want to. She takes good care of me. My brother drives me to school and work. They're great.

Review: Lessons 35–37

A

Yesterday, I had a very bad day because I overslept. My alarm clock didn't ring, and I didn't wake up at 6:30. I woke up at 8:15! I got dressed very fast and went to work. I didn't eat breakfast and I didn't comb my hair. When I got to work, I was very nervous. My boss was mad. She asked me, "Where were you this morning? Why did you get here so late?"

Lesson 38

A

Lily: We had a lot of fun when we were young. Do you remember when we went camping?
Ron: Of course! It was great. We went to the mountains and stayed in a beautiful campground. I remember we went hiking and swimming and had a great time.
Lily: We went to the mountains in the winter, too. We went skiing and ice skating. We were very active and athletic when we were young.
Ron: We're still active now. We go bowling every Friday night and we go dancing every Saturday night. And on Sundays, we go to the park. That's pretty good for people who are eighty!

Lesson 39

A

Interviewer: Do reporters and photographers follow you a lot?
Antonio: Yes, all the time. They follow us to the store, they follow us to the movies, they follow us home. They follow us everywhere.
Julia: Last month we took a trip. We went to Spain. We went to the mountains and we went to the beach. But there were always people with cameras.
Interviewer: Did you ask them to go away?
Julia: Yes, but they didn't listen. And when we got home, there were reporters in front of our house. I cried.
Antonio: I remember. You ran upstairs and went to bed. But I went outside and talked to the reporters.
Interviewer: Why?
Antonio: Well, because I like being famous, and I like to see my picture in magazines.

Lesson 40

A

Hi, I'm Molly. Every afternoon, I babysit Amanda (she's eight) and Davy (he's five). Every day after school, I pick up Amanda and Davy from their school. They wait for me in the schoolyard. Then we walk to their house and I take care of them until 6:00. Their mom comes home at 6:00. She's a single parent and she needs my help.

When we get to their house, the kids always ask me for a snack. I give them each two cookies and a glass of milk. Their mom calls them at 3:30 and they talk about their day. Davy always wants to talk to her first, so Amanda has to wait.

Davy usually brings home some pictures. Amanda and I look at them and we ask Davy a lot of questions about his pictures and about his day. Then Amanda talks about her day at school and we listen to her.

I like my job a lot, and I'm saving money for college. And the kids are great. I really like them.

Lesson 41

A

Lynn, Amanda, and Davy are usually very busy. On weekday mornings, Lynn takes a shower and then she makes breakfast. While the kids have breakfast, she makes the beds. Then she does the dishes. She takes good care of her children and her home.

Lynn takes the children to school, and then she takes the train to work. She takes a break at 10:00, and at 12:00 she has lunch. Then she takes a walk in the park.

In the afternoon, Molly, the babysitter, picks Amanda and Davy up from school. They walk home. They don't take the bus. Davy doesn't take a nap after school, but he rests because he's tired. Amanda does her homework. When Amanda makes mistakes, Molly helps her.

In the evening, Lynn makes dinner. Sometimes Lynn does laundry after dinner. Amanda takes a shower and Davy takes a bath. After Lynn reads to the children, she does the dishes and goes to bed.

Review: Lessons 38–41

A

Every summer when we were children, my sister and I visited our grandparents in the country. They took care of us for the summer. The day we arrived at their house was always the most exciting. When we got there, we had lunch and talked about our lives in the city. After lunch, we took a nap because it was very hot. When we woke up, we went to the lake and went swimming. Almost every day was like this, and we had a great time.

Lesson 42

A

1. Amy: Linda, what are you going to get Jenny?
   Linda: Marcia, Fran and I are going to get a stroller.
2. Linda: Amy, how about you?
   Amy: I'm probably going to buy some cute baby clothes.
3. Lily: Tina, what are you going to buy?
   Tina: I'm not going to buy a present. I'm going to make a blanket.
4. Linda: Lily, how about you and Sam?
   Lily: Sam and I are not going to buy a present. We're going to build a crib.
5. Linda: Andrea and Andy?

Andrea: We're going to get a car seat.

Lesson 43

A

Sam: Did you call Jenny? When are we going to visit?
Lily: Yes, I called her. We can visit between 4:00 and 7:00.
Sam: Great. How's Kenny? Is he going to be there?
Lily: Yes, I think so. He's so happy.
Sam: I know. But he needs to get some sleep now because he's going to be very tired when the baby comes home.
Lily: When are you going to talk to him?
Sam: I'm going to call him right now.
Lily: That's a good idea. Here's the number.

Lesson 44

A

Grandmother: Look at her big brown eyes. I think she'll be very beautiful.
Grandfather: But she probably won't be tall. Kenny and Jenny aren't very tall.
GM: She won't be tall, but she'll be healthy and beautiful.
GF: I'm sure she will be. But she won't look like our Jenny. See-she has Kenny's brown eyes and blonde hair.
GM: That's true. She'll look like Kenny. And she'll have a wonderful life. Jenny and Kenny love to travel, and Katie will, too.
GF: How many languages do you think Katie will speak?
GM: Oh, probably about five.
GF: Five? Well, why not! And I think she'll be a doctor.
GM: Just like you!
GF: Why not? And one last prediction--I think she'll have a little brother or sister in about two years.

Lesson 45

A

Katie: Mom, can we go to a party on Saturday night?
Mom: Where will it be?
Katie: At Sara's house.
Mom: What time will it be?
Katie: I think it'll be around 7:30 or 8:00 to midnight.
Mom: Who will be there?
Jamie: Our friends from school.
Mom: Will Sara's parents be home?
Katie: Uh-huh.
Mom: Well, you and Jamie can go, but you need to be home by 11:00.
Jamie: But mom…the party won't be over!
Mom: Midnight is too late. How will you get there?
Jamie: We'll take the bus.
Mom: OK. But remember--you need to be home by 11:00!

Lesson 46

A

1. This is going to be a great party.
2. We'll have a great time tonight.
3. A: This box of CDs is heavy!
   B: I'll help you carry it.
4. I'm going to get something to eat.
5. I think we're going to have trouble with mom and dad if we're late.
6. I'm going to sit outside for a while. It's hot in here.
7. A: I forgot my jacket.
   B: I'll get it.
8. A: Thanks for the party, Sara. I'll call you tomorrow.

Review: Lessons 42–46

A

Grace lives in Korea right now. She's going to study English in the U.S. next year. She's going to live with her friend, Gabriela.

Gabriela is from Argentina. Grace and Gabriela will probably speak only English together because Grace doesn't know Spanish, and Gabriela doesn't know Korean. They probably won't understand each other all the time, but they will try to communicate.

Lesson 47

A

I'd like to tell you about two very different brothers, Jeff and Martin. Jeff is a genius. He can do complicated math problems in his head. He can remember everything he reads. When he was only two years old, he could read. When he was three years old, he could write. He graduated from college when he was eighteen.

Martin is different. He isn't a genius. He can't do math problems in his head, and he can't remember everything he reads. When he was two years old, he couldn't read, and when he was three, he couldn't write. But he is very athletic. He can run very, very fast. He can play soccer and baseball very well. Jeff isn't athletic. He can't run fast and he can't play soccer or baseball well.

Lesson 48

A

I love living in New York City. I can walk to work and I can walk to the store. I don't need a car--I can take the subway or a bus or a taxi if I need to go somewhere far. I can go to the movies whenever I want. And I can go to a Broadway show tonight.

When I was a child, I loved living on a farm in the country. It was very quiet. At night I could hear all the sounds of the insects and animals and I could see so many stars in the sky. I could ride my horse around the farm

for hours. But I couldn't walk to school or to my friends' houses because it was too far.

In New York I can't have the quiet life I had on the farm. But I like life in the city. And when I need a quiet vacation, I can visit my parents.

Lesson 49

A

Part 1
Teacher: O.K. everyone. The test is tomorrow. I hope you all meet with your study groups this afternoon. Do you have any questions about the test?
Student 1: Can we use a dictionary during the test?
Teacher: No, you can't use a dictionary. But don't worry. You know all the words.
Student 2: Can we write in pencil?
Teacher: No, I want you to use a pen.
Student 3: Can we leave when we're done?
Teacher: Yes, you can leave. But be sure to write down the homework before you leave.
Student 4: I have a question...is the test going to be easy?
Teacher: Yes, it is...if you study!

Part 2
Joe: What are you reading?
May: Oh, these are some of my notes. I wrote them last night.
Joe: Could I see them?
May: Sure.
Joe: Wow! You studied a lot for this test!
May: Six hours. I'm really nervous.
Joe: I am, too. And I forgot my dictionary. Can I borrow yours?
May: The teacher said we can't use a dictionary during the test.
Joe: Oh, that's right. Look, here he is...Hi Mr. Seeger. Can we go home now?
Teacher: Very funny, Joe. Just relax. You'll do fine on the test.

Review: Lessons 47–49

A

Matt: You play the piano really well, Linda
Linda: Thanks, Matt. Can you play the piano?
Matt: No. I could play when I was young, but I can't play anymore.
Linda: Can you play any other instruments?
Matt: Yes, I can play the guitar and the drums. How about you?
Linda: I can't play the drums, but I can play the guitar.
Matt: Can you sing?
Linda: No, my sister can sing, but I can't sing at all. Can you sing?
Matt: Well, I thought I could sing when I was a teenager. I sang all the time. But I was really terrible. My friends and family begged me to stop.

Lesson 50

A

Dear Annie,
I need your advice. I'm getting married next year. My fiancé and I want a small wedding, but my parents want a big wedding. My older sister had a small wedding, so now they want to give me a big party. Should I have a big wedding? Should I listen to my parents?
Unhappy Melanie in Seattle

Dear Unhappy Melanie,
Your wedding is very special. I think you should talk to your parents. They should know what you want. You shouldn't keep your feelings a secret. It's your wedding, so you and your fiancé should have the wedding you want. Good luck to you!
Annie

Lesson 51

A

1. I'm sorry I have to be absent tomorrow. I have to take my

daughter to the doctor. She has to have surgery.

2. I'm sorry I missed work yesterday. I had to go to traffic court.

3. I'm sorry I can't go to the movies with you. I have to study for a test.

4. I was absent yesterday because I had to go to the doctor. Can I have the handout?

5. I can't go to the party because I have to pick my mom up at the airport.

6. I'm sorry I had to leave the office early yesterday. My son got sick at school and I had to pick him up.

7. I couldn't go out to dinner with you because I had to stay late at work.

Lesson 52

A

Hmmm. I have to get up early tomorrow so I should set my alarm for 7:30. I shouldn't sleep late. I have a lot to do before the party tomorrow night. I'm going to see Gina, and I want to look good. I really like her. I think I should get a haircut because my hair looks terrible. Maybe she'll see my car, so I should go to the car wash. My car is really dirty.

But before I do all that, I have to do my taxes because I have to mail them on Monday. And I have to do my laundry because I have nothing to wear. Maybe I should set my alarm for 6:30. Hmm…No, I don't have to get up at 6:30. That's too early. I should sleep. I'll get up at 7:30.

Review: Lessons 50–52

A

My cousin, Alex, is going to arrive at 9:00 tonight. I have to pick him up at the airport. I don't have a car, so I have to borrow my friend's car. This is Alex's first trip here, so I think I should give him a tour tomorrow. We should walk around downtown and have lunch. I'm lucky that tomorrow is Sunday and I don't have to work. On Monday, Alex is going to start English classes.

Lesson 53

A

Reporter: Congratulations Carmen! You're going to start college in August, but what are you going to do this summer?
Carmen: Well, I have a summer job at a bookstore. I need to make some money for college.
Reporter: Are you planning to live in a dorm?
Carmen: Yes. And my best friend and I decided to be roommates.
Reporter: That sounds great.
Carmen: Uh-huh. We both like to have a good time, but we also want to be good students. I want to get good grades so I can go to law school.
Reporter: Well, I wish you luck! … Uh, I see here that the university is a hundred miles away. Do you think you're going to miss your family a lot?
Carmen: Oh, yes! I'm going to try to visit them once a month. I love to be with my family. And I'm planning to e-mail my sister every day because we're so close.
Reporter: That sounds like a good plan. It was great talking to you. Good luck in school.
Carmen: Thanks a lot.

Lesson 54

A

Nick: Sophie, what do you want to order?
Sophie: I want a hamburger.
Nick: You had a hamburger yesterday. How about chicken salad?
Sophie: I like chicken salad, but today I would like to have a ham-

burger. And French fries.
Nick: No fries today, Sophie. You should have a salad. But you can have a hamburger.
Sophie: OK, Daddy. What are you going to have?
Nick: I think I would like the chicken salad. Oh, here's the waitress.
Waitress: Hi. Are you ready to order?
Nick: Yes, my daughter would like a hamburger.
Waitress: With fries?
Nick: No. She would like a small salad. And a lemonade.
Sophie: Oh, good. I like lemonade a lot.
Waitress: I like it, too. And how about you?
Nick: I would like the chicken salad and some iced tea.

Lesson 55

A

Nicole: Hello.
Greg: Hi, Nicole? This is Greg -- I'm Jill's brother.
Nicole: Oh, hi Greg! How are you?
Greg: Pretty good. Uh, I got your number from Jill. I was wondering…would you like to have dinner on Friday night?
Nicole: I'm sorry, but I can't Friday night. How about Saturday night?
Greg: Saturday's fine. What do you like to eat?
Nicole: I like everything. Mexican, Thai, Vietnamese, Indian, Italian…
Greg: Do you like Moroccan food?
Nicole: Yes, I do. I love it!
Greg: Well, there's a really good Moroccan restaurant in the city. They have great food and music. Would you like to try that?
Nicole: Sure. It sounds great.
Greg: OK. I'll pick you up at 7:00.
Nicole: Perfect. See you on Saturday. Bye.

Review: Lessons 53–55

A

Martin: Hi. How can I help you?
Emily: I'd like to get a map of San Francisco.
Martin: Sure, here you are. Would you like anything else?
Emily: Yes. We're planning to go to L.A. tomorrow, so we want to see a lot of San Francisco in one day. What do you think we should do?
Martin: I think you should take a bus tour. You'll like it because you'll see a lot in one day. Here's the information. You should be at the bus stop by 10:00.
Emily: Thanks. That's a great idea.

Lesson 56

A

OK, children Simon says "Close your eyes." Simon says "Touch your knees. Touch your toes." Sorry, Laura. I didn't say "Simon Says." Please sit down.

OK, everyone. Simon says "Put your right hand on your head." Simon says "Stand on your left foot." Simon says "Jump three times. Turn around three times." Sam, please sit down. I didn't say "Simon says."

Ready? Simon says "Clap your hands." Simon says "Open your mouth. Cover your ears." Billy, please sit down. Congratulations, Rebecca! You're the winner!

Lesson 57

A

1. Larry: It's a beautiful day. Let's go swimming in the river.
   Barry: Ah, let's not go swimming in the river. The water's cold. Let's take a walk.
   Harry: No, Phil. I agree with Larry. Let's go swimming.
2. Harry: That was a great hike. Now I'm really hungry. Let's eat!

Barry: But we ate two hours ago. Let's eat later.
   Larry: I'm hungry, too. I always get hungry after I go hiking. Let's eat now!
3. Harry: Let's go into town and go to the movies.
   Larry: No, Harry! We're camping. I don't want to go into town.
   Barry: I agree with Larry. Let's not go into town. Let's stay here.
4. Larry: It's a beautiful night. Let's make a campfire.
   Harry: Let's not make a campfire again. We made one last night.
   Barry: Yeah, let's just go to sleep. It's late, and I'm tired.
5. Barry: Let's go talk to those girls over there.
   Larry: Where? Oh, I see them. Uh…I can't go. I'm too shy.
   Harry: You're not too shy. Come on. Let's go and say hello.

Lesson 58

A

1. Bill: How's your dinner?
   Ruby: The chicken is too spicy! I can't eat it!
2. Bill: Wow! This chicken is very spicy!
   Ruby: Do you want to order something else?
   Bill: No! I love spicy food.
3. Ruby: Why aren't you eating?
   Bill: My soup is too hot. I can't eat it right now.
4. Ruby: How was the meeting?
   Bill: It was very long, but it was OK.
5. Ruby: I want to go home.
   Bill: Why?
   Ruby: This party is too noisy and crowded.
6. Ruby: How's the party?
   Bill: It's very noisy and crowded, but I'm having a great time.

7. Ruby: Let's go out to dinner.
   Bill: I'm sorry, I can't. I'm too tired. I can't go out.
8. Ruby: Let's go out to dinner.
   Bill: Good idea! I'm very tired, and I don't want to cook.

Lesson 59

A

Molly: What's wrong?
Alice: I want to move.
Molly: Why?
Alice: It's my roommates. I can't study because there are always too many people in our apartment. And I can't sleep because they make too much noise.
Molly: That's terrible.
Alice: And they never clean up. There are always a lot of dirty dishes in the sink.
And they buy too much junk food--candy and chips and sodas.
Molly: You need to talk to them! You have a lot of problems, but maybe your roommates can try to change.
Alice: I don't think so. I need to find a new apartment.
Molly: Do you want to move in with me?

Review: Lessons 56–59

A

OK. Let's make scrambled eggs! It's very easy. This recipe is for two or three people.
First, heat some oil or butter in a pan. Don't use too much.
Then, beat six eggs with a fork.
Then, add some milk.
Next, pour the eggs into the pan. Move the eggs around with a spoon.
Don't forget to add some salt and pepper. Eat your eggs with toast and you'll have the perfect breakfast!

Lesson 60

A

1. old
2. lazy
3. beautiful
4. cheap
5. ugly
6. expensive
7. sad
8. noisy
9. interesting
10. smart

Lesson 61

A

Laura: Can I see a picture of your family?
Steve: Sure…here's one. It's from our family reunion last summer. This is my father and this is my uncle.
Laura: Who's older?
Steve: My father's older. He's 61 and my uncle is 58. And here's my father's sister. She's younger than they are. I think she's 55.
Laura: Do you have any cousins?
Steve: Do I have any cousins? I think I have about thirty! Here's Jeff--He learned to read when he was only two years old. He's really intelligent.
Laura: Is he more intelligent than you?
Steve: Well…probably. But I'm more interesting than he is. And I'm more handsome.

Lesson 62

A

1. old
2. lazy
3. beautiful
4. cheap
5. ugly
6. expensive
7. sad
8. noisy
9. interesting
10. smart

Lesson 63

A

1. The biggest country in the world is Russia. Canada is the second biggest, and the United States is the third biggest.
2. The smallest country in the world is Vatican City. Many people think it's in Italy, but Vatican City IS a country.
3. The most populated country is China. It had 1,286,975, 468 people in 2003.
4. In 2003, Mexico City had between eight and nine million people, but the most populated city in the world is Bombay, India. Bombay had over 12 million people in 2003.
5. The Atlantic Ocean is big, but the Pacific Ocean is bigger. The Pacific covers more than 32% of the Earth, so it is the biggest ocean in the world.
6. The Amazon River has more water than the Nile River, but the Nile is the longest river in the world.

Lesson 64

A

That's Chris Leon from the Canadian team. He's the fastest skier from Canada. He can ski faster than his father, who was an Olympic champion many years ago.

Mark Brewer is a speed skater. He's the oldest skater on his team, but he's the strongest and the fastest. I met Mark a few years ago and really enjoyed talking to him. He's the funniest, the friendliest and the most interesting athlete I know. Maybe that's why he's the most popular athlete in Canada. He's more popular than movie stars!

Review: Lessons 60–64

A

1. Student 1: What's harder for you? English grammar or spelling?
   Student 2: Spelling. Spelling is the hardest thing for me to learn.
2. Student 1: What's more difficult for you? Understanding what you hear, or speaking?
   Student 2: Understanding what I hear. For me, speaking English is easier than understanding it.
3. Student 1: What's the easiest for you? Reading, writing or speaking?
   Student 2: For me, the easiest is reading. It's very hard for me to write and speak English.

Index